The Complete Offensive System for Youth Football:
A Guide to Implementing a Hurry-Up-No-Huddle Spread Offense

Pat Moss

First Printing: 2016

ISBN 978-1-329-8711-5

Pat Moss
2202 Wellington Plantation Drive
Little Rock, Arkansas 72211

Dedication

To my wife and children who inspire me to be a better husband, father, and person – Colleen, Hudson, Regan, Dylan, Addison, Quinn and Ryan-Lucy.

Table of Contents

Preface

We parents want to be good examples and help our children learn something about what is important in life, like having character and honoring teamwork. A father and a good coach can inspire kids and help teach those important values. I recall my own father, who was a genuine inspiration.

With a chewed up cigar as a conductor's wand, my father would bark out a play, then park the mauled tobacco nub back into the corner of his mouth. With great passion he would call-out a player who made some mistake, and then he would put his arm around that same player's shoulder and gently teach him how not to make it again. He would encourage those who weren't athletically blessed and humble those who were.

I was lucky to grow up with a father who played and knew the game of football. But he never spoke of himself or what he accomplished, because he didn't coach to make it about himself. When he coached, it was about the kids and to an even larger degree, his sons.

Most dads never truly know the positive impact they have on their children. Most coaches don't know either and in many cases, they are one and the same.

I wrote this book for you dads who, after spending a long day at work or for-going a much-deserved nap on the weekend, load your kids in the car to spend the next few hours coaching football. This is for you dads who would love to call out names, plays, encouragements, and mistakes, but you aren't sure how to get started coaching a Hurry-Up-No-Huddle spread offense. This book, I hope, will be a resource that provides answers to questions and helps you avoid some mistakes. Most of all, I hope it helps you to be an inspiration.

Acknowledgements

I would like to thank the numerous dads and friends with whom I have had the good fortune to coach and learn especially Chris Keylon, John McCuistion, Trey Bell, and Ty Vaughn. I would also like to thank my family without whose help, guidance, and criticism, this book would never have been completed. Lastly, I would like to thank my mom. She's an amazing educator, and any grammatical mistakes that occur in this book aren't because she didn't try and teach me; rather, I was likely daydreaming at the time.

Introduction

You are a new offensive coach of the great game of football and don't know how to get started. Perhaps you are very defensive-minded and don't know much about offenses, particularly the popular spread Hurry-Up-No-Huddle schemes. You have questions that need answers. This book should help answer some of those questions.

Before we go further, I should probably say for whom this book is and isn't written. First, who would benefit from reading my book:

- o People who want to coach a youth football team in their spare time.
- o Coaches of teams that practice two to three times a week and have a weekly game.
- o People who have a good knowledge of football, but their primary job is not being a coach.
- o Coaches of younger players aged 8 to about 14.

That having been said, this book does include material that can be used by full-time coaches or for those who coach older teams that can execute more complicated schemes, but those are not the target reading audiences. The material has been purposely and greatly simplified to be effective for younger players of teams coached by volunteers.

This book has three major goals:

- o To help inexperienced, youth, head coaches focus on being the "right" kind of coach (Greater explanation comes later).

- o To outline a Hurry Up No Huddle (HUNH) play-calling system that is fast and easy to comprehend by young players.

- o To provide an offensive scheme that young players can learn and execute effectively:

    - Is learned quickly.

    - Deceives the opponents.

- Scores a lot of points.

- Provides a fun game.

- Runs plays similar to what more advanced levels might execute.

The scope of this book is not to detail every possible position technique, drill, or offensive line-blocking technique. Neither does it offer how to counter every defensive attack, or how to evaluate talent; I made the assumption that you have a good and basic knowledge of football and can handle and use that knowledge at the youth level. This book presents a very good, simple, and proven offensive system; additionally, it is also designed to provide general guidance on details that are sometimes overlooked or not considered. The material will help you to simplify and make practices more effective, to help you properly plan, and mostly to provide specific and detailed guidance to implement a Hurry-Up-No-Huddle (HUNH) spread offensive system for youth.

Being the Right Kind of Coach

Being a good coach means being "the right kind" of coach. Kids have certain psychological needs and a good coach meets those needs.

We should always be aware that kids play football because they want to have fun. There will be a few who might be lazy and their parents are pushing them to do something, to be active. There might even be a few who are being pushed because their parents "live the game through their children." In either case, you can't do anything about those reasons, because in the end, even those kids still want to have fun.

Coaches, essentially, should satisfy four needs for kids to have fun:

o Appreciate each player.

o Listen to and try to understand each player.

o Challenge each player.

o Communicate that each player is a part of something bigger than himself.

Meeting these needs helps lead to overall success; when the players are having fun, success usually follows.

To be Appreciated

The easiest way to show appreciation is to demonstrate respect. That means, when a player makes a mistake, don't get personal. Call out mistakes and help everyone understand the error. But, don't call any player "stupid" or "lazy" or an "idiot" or any other name. If a player makes a mistake and you yell out the mistake, be sure to then go to him calmly and explain what he did and how to correct it.

The next way to show respect is to point out when a player does something well. We all know that it's certainly easier for coaches to point out the faults, but that has to happen, too. One of the worst postures a coach can take is to avoid pointing out a problem. These young players won't learn from their mistakes if the mistakes aren't identified. When at all possible, however, accent the positives more than the negatives.

You will also want to make sure all positions are considered when pointing out positives. It's easy to praise a great pass from a quarterback, a great run from a running back, or a great catch from a tight-end or wide receiver. But, linemen do great things, too.

Lastly, create a reward system in which players get decals for great performances. This is positive feedback and helps them know they are appreciated and noticed by their coach.

Be Heard and Understood

The second need all kids have is to "be heard and understood." It's easy as a coach to give the team its marching orders and wait for the results. But, when something doesn't go well, be sure to *ask the player what happened*; get his input.

Sometimes a player's response is, "I just missed the block" or "I dropped the ball on the exchange." As a coach, you should respect the honesty and personally accepting responsibility.

Sometimes, however, you might get a response like this one: "Well, we were lined up to run Arkansas Black out of the 21 formation. When we did that, the linebacker didn't slide out on the TE, but stayed over me to my right, so I wasn't sure who to block."

In that situation, it's our faults as coaches that he didn't know whom to block. The player provided some very good information that you can use to improve him and the team. Be sure to "playback" (e.g., repeat) what the player said to ensure you properly understood too. In this way you can be sure you know what to fix.

To be Challenged

One of the easiest needs to meet in football is to challenge a player. Ultimately, that's what coaches do: teach something new and then help the player learn it. Instilling your high-expectations in the team for the season (i.e., winning the championship) naturally challenges the players.

Meeting this need-to-be-challenged is almost "by default" in football; that is, it's the nature of the game to challenge players. Apply some techniques in order to maintain or even amp up this need throughout the season:

- o Demand perfect execution on every play, of every player, and at every position.

- o Continue to teach new plays for both offense and defense.

- o Continue to work on position techniques; push the players to be excellent and mistake free.

- o Let players try different positions from time to time.

To be a Part of Something Bigger than Themselves

The essence of "team" is to have individuals believe that they are a part of something bigger than themselves. Players should feel as integrated and important parts of the overall success of the team, regardless of their position or role.

I have a few strategies to make sure each player is a part of the "bigger picture" and a part of the team:

- o Create a buddy system between the older, more experienced players and the new, inexperienced players – the experienced player's job is to look after the new player and help him learn the game.

- o While "healthy conflict" may be motivational, we do not allow physical fights. Period. If players get into fights (and it happens, it's football), we make them hold hands. Trust me, when two boys have to hold hands, it's pretty embarrassing. However, nearly every time we do this, everyone starts laughing – together – not making fun of the hand-holders; they are laughing too, but at how funny and stupid the whole situation is. We then ask them to apologize to each other.

- o We do not allow "bad-mouthing" between teammates. When something goes wrong, there are no excuses or blaming. For example, when there is a fumble, if either the QB or RB blames the other one, the one who blames has to run a lap. If they both say, "I messed that up," then we thank them for owning the problem, and go to the next play. It is over. It is the coach's job to explain the error; it is his job to take the responsibility.

o Carefully explain how each person's position is important and necessary to the team's success. We say to the team, "There are eleven positions on both sides of the ball; if one of them wasn't important, there would be only ten."

o Let the team know that they have a chance to be part of something very special. They have an opportunity to play and do great things as a team, and it is a privilege to be on the team.

In conclusion, meeting the four needs of the players isn't really that difficult but does require some practice. Try these ideas at home in your own way – your success with these skills can make all the difference on the field.

Things that are Missed

In this chapter I will focus on details that new coaches often over-look or don't place proper emphasis. More often than not, new coaches want to go straight to coaching the offense or defense without considering a few qualities that separate good teams from great. This chapter's goal is to help you avoid those pitfalls.

Fundamentals First, Defense Second

Football is about blocking, tackling, and protecting the football. If the team doesn't do these three things properly, consistently, and well, you won't win many games; therefore, your team should be per-fecting these skills at every practice. Your first couple of practices should place even *more* emphasis on these fundamentals. There are volumes of great drill books and videos that can help you coach these aspects of your team and some helpful ones are listed in the appendix.

Second to fundamentals is a focus on the defense before the of-fense. There are some truths in football and this is one of them: "Defense wins championships." You must have a good defense to consistently win games.

At your first practice, you will want to focus on the defense after introductions and blocking/tackling drills. If you start out working on offense first, you'll end up with little time at the end of your first practice for defense; a youth-level defense just isn't as complicated as a youth-level offense. You will lose too much time trying to teach just one simple play; therefore, focus on tackling, taking proper pur-suit angles, something that almost every youth team neglects, and executing defensive assignments. You won't be sorry.

The Most Important Position

Without a doubt, one of the most difficult jobs of a new coach is selecting the best player for each position. In addition to evaluating skills, you will need to consider personality, attitude, commitment, drive, desire and unfortunately, sometimes even politics.

The good news is that at the youth level, many positions are generally equal to others in terms of skills required to be successful. An exception, obviously, is the quarterback; however, there is one very specific assessment that should be made with care – the Center. If the Center can't snap the ball cleanly back to the QB, then the team won't be able to run any plays successfully.

Successfully snapping the ball means the timing of the play is correct and that there is significantly less chance for a fumble from the ball going over the QB's head or to his side. Take the time to really evaluate the center. As players are being evaluated for this position and are making snaps, these things should be considered, both for a potential starter and his backup:

o Can the would-be Center place the ball reasonably well at the QB's mid section?

o Does he avoid hesitating when you say "hut" or "go"?

o Can he hike the ball without looking through his legs or over his shoulders? If he needs to look through his legs or over his shoulder, he may still be an effective Center provided he can still make a block on the opposing defensive player. You will need to weigh this ability against the other requirements listed.

o Can the player still make a good snap *and* move forward if he is required to make a block after the snap?

The Center is key, so spend adequate time to identify this player and his backup.

The Passing Game in Youth Football

The ability to successfully and consistently pass is prized for all QB's, but it isn't completely necessary in all systems. Think Georgia Tech and Paul Johnson's Flexbone offense. Neither is it required at the youth level. I highly discourage coaches from trying to pass more than 20% of the called plays at the younger youth level, say under 12 years old. Older teams can pass more often, which will be discussed in another chapter. That being said, a team must pass a few times a game, and the system presented in the book will generally lead to success if followed.

Even though you aren't passing much, you still need to assess and try to find a QB who can pass reasonably well. If one wasn't assigned at your draft, then you will have to make a quick assessment out of all your players. This assessment should consist of using players of a medium build, who are fast, smart and at least one of the top 10 tallest on the team if possible.

When considering a player for QB, there are two additional evaluations to consider. The first and most important is to see if the QB can pass on the run. Second, is his general passing ability from the shotgun making a 3-step drop. Feel free to set up the evaluation drills as you best see fit.

Practice Plans

In Sun Tzu's book, *The Art of War*[1], he makes the claim that the battle is won before it is even fought. That claim is as true in sports as it is in military action - excellent planning and practice will often lead to victory on the field.

As a coach you will need to have your practices planned in advance and communicated to your assistant coaches. All the coaches need to clearly understand the expectation for each practice. There is little worse for a kid than to come to a disorganized practice. Those types of practices create confusion for the player, frustration for their parents, and poor results for a team.

There are as many schools of thought about proper practice plans as there are for different offenses. However, generally you'll want these elements:

o   Warm up - stretching and running

o   Position and/or squad break outs – skills and drills that focus
    on linemen (offense and defense), wide-receivers,
    quarterbacks, running backs, and defensive backs or offensive
    and defensive squad breakouts.

---

[1] Minford, John *The Art of War*. trans. New York: Viking. 2002. Print.

o   Breaks – water and sometimes instruction (e.g., play diagramming)

o   Scrimmage

o   Cool down and discussion

Since you are running a HUNH offense, practices should have the same speed and intensity as in a game. Players should run to each drill and position or squad breakout. Everything should be timed and one coach should be assigned to make sure you stick to that time. Always practice the HUNH system, even when scrimmaging against your own team. Teach players to do actions like this so in the game you can get your teamed lined up as quickly as possible:

o   Hand the ball to the official after the play is whistled dead. This can be practiced.

o   Have the center locate the ball after the play and run to its placement.

o   Have players, after they are lined up or after the play, always turn towards the coaches or the side line to see what play will be called.

Setting Ground Rules

Here's a truth - you are coaching players, but to some small degree also the parents. Most parents are well-meaning and don't want to cause problems. Unfortunately, there's often one or two, well, to put it mildly, "more difficult" people that you'll encounter. Having ground rules up front helps prevent a bad situation. Ground rules also set expectations for the players and even the coaches.

These ground rules are to be distributed the first day of practice. Here are a few of ours:

o   Fighting between (or among) teammates will not be tolerated.

o   Bad-mouthing or blaming teammates will not be tolerated.

- o Players should be at all practices and on-time. If a player can't make it or will be late, he should contact one of the coaches.

- o Coaches are the only adults allowed on the practice and game fields.

- o Coaches *only* will handle any problems with officiating during a game, should problems arise.

- o Coaches will assign positions for all players. Those positions may change or stay the same for the season. While they will do their best to let everyone try a position, coaches designate the best positions for both player and team success.

- o Players should bring their own water to practices. Coaches will provide water for the games.

Feel free to add or modify as these are just some suggestions.

Background Checks

Our league has background checks for its coaches and assistants. In today's environment, this is a wise and prudent precaution and an effective way to protect the kids. If your league doesn't have back-ground checks, I highly suggest you implement them. Our league pays for the head coach and one assistant; team members pay for all others coaches, approximately $15 per additional coach.

Background checks are also a great excuse to keep "difficult" parents off the practice and game fields. Simply explain that only coaches are allowed on the fields because they are the adults who have been approved with background checks.

Choosing Assistants

More often than not, your assistant coach(s) will be the father of a friend of your son's or just a friend. Consider these qualities when choosing assistants:

o   Can they meet the four basic needs of each player outlined in Chapter 1?

o   Do they understand the game of football and the techniques to teach at each position?

o   Do they complement the areas you are weak; for example, if you are an "offensive coach" does an assistant understand the defense better than you?

o   Are they reliable – will their jobs or other commitments keep them from being at most practices and games?

o   Will they understand the offensive scheme/system and could they successfully call plays if you weren't able?

o   Can they "take charge" without waiting for your lead?

Everything Else

The final preparation you will need to make is so you can handle the little things that creep up during practices (i.e., equipment problems, cuts, hydration and etc.). Rather than providing a great amount of detail, here's simply a list:

o   First Aid Kit – basic bandages, tape, gauze plus a cold pack or two

o   Whistle – each coach should have one. I recommend the type with the rubber sleeve – the metal whistles can get hot hanging around your neck in the sun.

o   Practice Cones – at least eight (8)

o   Duct Tape and Sharpie – use this to label the front of each player's helmet with his first or last name

o   Dry Erase board, marker and cloth – small enough to carry around and diagram plays and to communicate adjustments

- o Extra equipment – claps and helmet parts, shoulder pad straps and clasps, chin straps, mouth pieces, screw drivers, both Phillips and Flat head. You will need to make repairs on the fly. Your league should provide most of these items (except maybe the screwdrivers).

- o Water Cooler – sized for enough water for an entire practice – *highly important*. No matter how many times you tell the kids to bring their own water, someone always forgets. Keeping everyone hydrated is more important than anything else you can do as a coach.

Now that we have discussed details that are often missed by a new coach, be sure to share them with other coaches on the team. In the next chapter we outline a Hurry-Up-No-Huddle play calling system that will be used to communicate the offense to the team.

A Hurry Up No Huddle Play Calling System

This chapter will focus on how the plays are communicated in our Hurry-Up-No-Huddle (HUNH) system. This chapter also provides a "high-level" overview of the play structures.

A fair amount of flexibility is possible in how you can tailor the system to work best for you. You are encouraged to change things up just a little bit so as to avoid other coaches' understanding what you are doing (this assumes they have read this book or something similar).

Our scheme is set up to be learned very quickly and is considered somewhat unconventional. There will be coaches who disagree with the approach and the scheme, and I respect their opinions. Overall kids are pretty smart and will likely pick up on whatever offensive scheme you want to introduce, *given enough time*. But, in many cases, coaches have very few practices, and only half of the time, those practices are working with the offense. I believe this system allows kids to understand a really fun scheme very quickly, and that's important especially in a HUNH Spread offense.

In this chapter we will develop these elements:

o   The play-calling system

o   Choosing play names and its importance

o   Directing the play - the "colored field"

o   Communicating the play, formation, and cadence with pictures, numbers, letters and colors

o   "Numbering" the hole – unconventional but easy to learn

o   Directing the FB to block

In this chapter I introduce concepts only, while the next chapter combines all of these elements into an offensive scheme. As you read, you will find how intimately each is tied to the other.

Play Calling System

There are several play-calling systems that can work with a HUNH Spread offense in youth football. An increasing number of football teams are using something similar as presented in this book. Overall, the general trend is that the called play is getting increasingly more simple. Our system is uncomplicated and highly effective.

Speed is one of the highest priorities for a HUNH team. Some coaches even believe the *pace* of execution is more important than exactly *what* is executed. The faster a play can be communicated and comprehended, the faster the execution.

Elements of the play-calling system:

o   Colors for the play direction

o   Pictures combined with colors to communicate plays and play direction

o   Numbers and colors to communicate formation and snap count

o   Letters for gaps

o   Signals for FB blocking

The Colored Field and Play Direction

Imagine that the football field is cut in half at the center position. The right half of the field is one color and the left is another. We use "Black" and "Red" for left and right, and it looks conceptually like what is illustrated in figure #1. For the remainder of the book, each half of the field will be referred to using these colors.

When calling a play, the direction of the play is determined by these colors. For example, if we call the play "Arkansas Red," the team knows that the play will be executed with the primary action going to the right side of the field.

At your first practice, you'll want to teach this concept. It is really simple and kids pick up on it quickly.

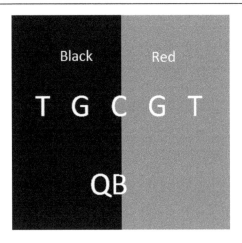

Figure #1

o   Have the team get in a group facing you the coach. You stand in front with your back to them, hold your right arm and say, "This half of the field is red."

o   Then, hold out your left arm and say, "This half of the field is black."

o   "When you look right you see Red; when you look left you see Black."

o   Then have the players repeat this back to you then and several more times over the practice.

Feel free to use colors that are relevant to you. We chose to use Black and Red because the local high school team uses these same colors. These colors will be also used in the next section when we create pictures which will be used to communicate the play.

Play Names

You will likely have very few practices. If you are lucky, you might have four practices to prepare your team for its first game; therefore, you want players to instinctively know what a play is doing just by how it is named. A coach could use a more standard nomenclature, but I believe that takes much more time to learn and makes execution less instinctual. We want players to act, not think; therefore, we chose play names carefully.

Some rules for creating play names so they are instinctive:
o   Make the name memorable.

o   Chose a name that can mean what it represents as much as possible; make an association.

o   Make the name relevant to the players. That is, don't use terms that their generation or age bracket won't understand (i.e., don't use "Bob Hope" or "Van Halen").

As an example, let's consider the play names we use and how they were chosen.

Every kid in our area knows SEC and other good NCAA football teams. Therefore, we chose play names that the kids know well, that are *memorable* and *relevant* based on those teams. The offensive scheme has three base plays (which will be explored more in detail in the next chapter). Our entire system is based on these three plays which we call "Arkansas," "Georgia," and "LSU." For the remainder of the book, I will refer to the plays as they are named in our system.

In teaching the play names, we say the following:
o   "When we run Arkansas, the runner *Razors* around the end" (Arkansas Razorbacks).

o   "When we run Georgia, the runner *Bulldogs* his way up the middle" (Georgia Bulldogs).

o   "When we run LSUUUUuuuu, whoooo's got the football? The QB, that's who." (LSU and "who" rhyme somewhat, no other reason for the association.)

The kids immediately pick up on the play name and then understand what will be happening. Any other play names can work; just be sure to develop an association between the name and the action on the field by using the rules above.

A few possible play names could be used:

- o Bear - "the runner bear claws up the middle"

- o Eagle – "the runner flies around the end"

- o Semi – the "QB's driving the truck"

- o Hulk – "the runner smashes his way up the middle"

- o Tony Stark – the "QB's is the Iron Man"

Play Cards

After a play is named based on the rules described, a picture is chosen to represent it. For example, here are five play pictures we use – "Arkansas Red," "Georgia Black," "Jet Black," "Jet Red," and "Jet Black Dive" (see if you can guess which picture applies to each play):

Once you decide on the pictures that represent your play names, the pictures are combined and displayed on large play-calling "cards." Consider this picture of a completed "Play Card" in figure #2:

Figure #2

As you can see in Figure #2, most pictures are printed with a colored background or border. The background or border color will be the "field colors" you read about earlier in this chapter; therefore, you will create pictures for the play names you choose, and place those pictures on either a Red or Black background, or on background colors you chose for your team. Look at Figure #2 above as an example:

o The Georgia "G" is printed with a black background. This represents "Georgia Black."

o The Arkansas "Razorback" appears twice, once with a red background and once with a black border. These pictures represent "Arkansas Red" and "Arkansas Black."

o The Auburn "AU" is printed twice, once with a red background and once with a black. These represent "Auburn Red" and "Auburn Black."

In the next chapter we will detail the actual plays and the use of the colors. Only one play in the entire scheme does not have a field color.

Here's how the play cards should be designed and made. Before you make the cards, be sure to read the next chapter. There are combinations of plays and special play signals which will need to be considered for each board. The pictures can be drawn by hand or created using resources listed in the appendix.

- o A picture is chosen to represent a play (see Figure #2). For example, we use an Arkansas Razorback to represent "Arkansas," The Georgia Bulldog logo "G" to represent "Georgia," the Auburn Tigers "AU" logo to represent "Auburn," and etc.

- o Each picture is created and printed on an 8.5" x 11" piece of paper in the "landscape" position and then pasted on a piece of corrugated board. Our board has six (6), but a board can have as few as four (4) plays. You really don't want more plays (pictures) on a card or the "cards" would be too big and hard to handle. Fewer than four plays and there's little deception in your play calling (more on that in later in this chapter). You will make your corrugated card large enough to fit four to six plays.

- o An 8.5" x 11" picture is the minimum size for a play. You might want larger depending on where you can call your plays (e.g., from the sideline versus on the field). If you call on the field, the standard paper size will work just fine. If you call from the sideline, a larger picture might be needed, in which case, you'll only get four on the card.

- o Several play-calling cards will be made in which the plays are seemingly placed randomly on the front and back of each card:

  - ▪ For example, in figure #2, we have "Air Raid," "Razorback Red," "Razorback Black," "Auburn Black," "Auburn Red," and "Georgia Black."

  - ▪ On the back of the same card we might have "Oregon Red," "Jet Red," "Jet Black Dive," "Auburn Red,"

> "Sponge Bob" (more on that later), and "Georgia Red."

- ▪ Other cards might have the same plays in a different sequence as well as other entirely different plays

o You will complete several cards – at least four and as many as six cards. This will give you a total of forty-eight plays: four cards with six plays on the front and six plays on the back, with seventy-two play combinations in total.

o Each card should be covered in clear contact paper to protect it from the elements.

Formation and Snap Count Cards

In addition to plays, there are several formations in the offensive scheme. These formations are communicated to the team on "Formation and Snap Count Cards" which are similar to "Play Cards."

In figure #3 you see the numbers "1" and "10" with a colored background, black and red respectively, as well as a picture of "Sponge Bob Square Pants." This is the "Formation and Snap Count Card." You will make these cards in the same fashion as you made the play cards. As with plays, the formation numbering system has detailed information in the next chapter.

Continuing with figure #3, formations are given as numbers. These numbers are printed and have a colored background. The background or border color for most of these cards uses a "field color" you read about earlier in this chapter. However, some formation #'s don't have a black or red background; remember, we use black and red as our field colors:

o A formation number that uses one of the "field colors" (i.e., black or red) indicates that the snap count is on one (1) or "hut." That is, the QB calls out, "Down, Set, Hut" and the ball is snapped.

- o Formation numbers with any color other than a "field" color means that the snap count is on two (2) or "hut, hut." That is, our QB calls out "Down, Set, Hut, Hut."
- o Any color, other than a field color, used as a formation number background indicates that the snap count is on, two, three, a "freeze play," or however you want to use it.

Some teams always snap the ball on the first "hut." Honestly, in youth football, with very young teams, there are good reasons for this. If that's the case in your system, you will still want the formations on different colored backgrounds as this creates deception. You just won't use the colors to communicate anything.

Figure #3

Here are the steps to construct the formation and snap count cards. As with the play cards, before making them, please read the next chapter. There are combinations of formations and special formation signals which will need to be considered.

- o Each formation number will be printed in as large a font as possible on an 8.5" x 11" piece of paper in the landscape orientation and then pasted on a piece of corrugated board.

- o Our formation cards have three (3) formations per each side of the card, but yours can have more; however, there are only a few formations, so you won't need to make as many cards, especially if you have more than three on a card. You really don't want more than three (3) to six (6) formations on a card or the "cards" would be too big and hard to handle. You also don't want fewer than three as there's less deception.

o An 8.5" x 11" picture is the minimum size for the formation number. You might want larger depending on where you can call your plays (e.g., from the sideline versus on the field). If you call on the field, the standard paper size will work just fine. If you call from the sideline, a larger picture might be needed.

o Additionally, several formation/cadence cards have the formations randomly placed on the front and back of each card:

  • For example, in the card above we have a "1," "Sponge Bob," and a "10."

  • On the back of the same card we might have "21," "20," and "22."

  • Other cards might have the same formations in a different sequence as well as other entirely different ones.

o You will make several cards – at least four and as many as six cards. This will give you a total of twenty –four (24) to thirty-six (36) formation-combinations. Each card should be covered in clear contact paper.

Gaps and Gap Cards

You might find the next part of our system a little unconvention-al. We have good reasons, and I believe in youth football, especially with very young teams, those reasons are even more valid. You don't have to implement this element of our system into yours; you can simply use the standard gap numbering scheme that's been used for the past 50 plus years and everything will work out just fine. Here is a picture showing how we name the gaps (see the figure #4):

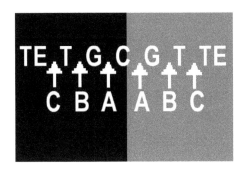

Figure #4

Gaps are simply given the letter "A," "B," or "C" as illustrated in figure #4. There is no "D" gap in our system. The running/blocking gap is communicated on a card just like the play and formation/snap count.

You will create a series of "Gap cards" with the letters "A," "B," and "C" on them. These cards are NOT printed and pasted on a large piece of corrugated board; rather, each letter is its own card.

The background color can stay "white"; however, another colored background can also be created. We're not big fans of using more colors for the simple reason that at some point too many colors can create confusion with the players.

We specify letters for gaps for a few reasons. Most of our kids play on both sides of the ball: offense and defense. Our defense gaps are typically identified as "A," "B," and etc. As the game wears on, players can get tired and remembering numbers on one side of the ball and letters on the other can be difficult. In addition, the slightly more complex numbering system most offenses use can slow down comprehension of the called play (e.g., a player, series, and gap such as "133"). We want the player to "see and know," not "see and think."

We'll get a little more into gaps in the next chapter, but as a primer, here's how it works:

o   The play is called. Let's say it is "Georgia Red."

o A gap is shown from the sideline with the letter "A."

o The offense then knows that the runner will be running through the "A" gap (e.g., between the Center and the Guard) on the "Red" (e.g., Right) side of the field.

o **It should be noted – that in all plays where a gap is not specified and the FB has not been given the signal to block, that the default gap is always "A" to the same side as the play's action.**

Gap cards are made in the same manner as the play and formation cards. That is, the letters A, B, and C will each be printed in very large font (as big as you can get on one page), in landscape format, on an 8.5" by 11" pieces of paper. That card will be glued to a piece of corrugated board, or it can be laminated in plastic.

Figure #5 shows a gap card:

Figure #5

If you choose to use the standard gap numbering system, make similar cards using *numbers* rather than *letters* (e.g., 0, 1, 2, 3, 4, and etc.).

FB Blocking

Lastly, there are two signals that the coaches give from the side-line to the Full Back (FB):

o The first signal is shown in figure #5. This signals the FB to block. This is signaled in our system as "crossed arms" by the coach calling the play. When given this signal, the FB will become a lead blocker for the primary ball carrier and will not receive a fake handoff.

o   The second signal shown in figures #6 and #7 is the direction the FB is to block – either to the right or to the left ("Red" or "Black") signaled by extending the left or right arm. The play and this signal will also dictate the FB's direction to block as described in later chapters.

Figures #5, #6 and #7 demonstrate the signals that can be used (feel free to use whatever makes the most sense for your team):

Figure #5   **Figure #6**   **Figure #7**

Putting it All Together

1) As an example, you call the play, "1 Arkansas Black FB Black on 1." You (or another coach) do this by holding up the play card with your hand touching the Razorback on the black background (figure #8). **Your hand on the play picture is the called play signal.**

2) Another coach or player holds up the formation card with his hand touching the "1" card (figure #9) with a red or black background. **A hand on the formation number is the called formation and snap count signal.**

3) A gap card will also be held up (figure #10) by another coach or player.

4) The FB is signaled (by the coach who called the play) in pictures #11 and #12 to block to the left or "Black" side through the called "B" gap.

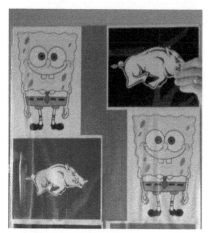

Figure #8   **Figure #9**

Figure #10

Figure #11   **Figure #12**

The next few figures provide examples of how other plays are called in the system. The plays are "21 Auburn Black," "12 Jet Black FB Black on 2," and "11 Georgia Red Bob." At this point don't worry about what the play actually is as you will learn about them in the next few chapters. Simply use these pictures as examples of how plays are communicated to your team.

21 Auburn Black

Notes for "21 Auburn Black":
- The use of the number "32" other than a gap designation isn't needed. This is a form of deception and will be explained in the next section.
- No FB has been signaled to block
- The "21" has a "red" background, so the snap count is on "1."

12 Jet Black FB Black on 2

Notes for "12 Jet Black FB Black on 2":
- The use of the number "45" other than a gap designation isn't needed. This is a form of deception and will be explained in the next section.
- The "12" has a "green" background which isn't a field color. Therefore, the snap count is on "2."

11 Georgia Red Bob C

Notes for "11 Georgia Bob Red C":
- The FB will lead through the "C" gap.
- The "11" has a "red" background.

Play Calling Procedure

The plays are called from either behind the players (if coaches are allowed on the field) or from the sideline. When the players first take the field on offense, the team will be given the first play before they sprint to the line of scrimmage. After the first play ends, several actions occur:

1) The player who had the ball last hands it to the closest official.

2) All offensive linemen (Center, Guards and Tackles) will sprint up to where the official spots the ball. They will remain in a two-point stance and turn towards the side-line.

3) The Tight-Ends, Wings, and Quarterback (skill players) will move towards the new line of scrimmage with their eyes towards the side-line.

4) The skill players will then align themselves per the formation and play call.

5) The players should wait just long enough for the coach to signal the play and then put the play call card down.

6) The Quarterback will wait for everyone to be aligned and then go into his cadence (e.g., "Down, Set, Blue 2, Blue 2, Hut").

Steps 1 through 6 should be practiced until perfect and there is little delay between the previous down and the snap of the ball.

When signaling plays, enlist at least three coaches/players, but it is preferable you use four. Another way to involve players in the team's success is for them to help signal plays. The steps for signaling plays are the following:

1) One coach will signal the play – this may require him to signal a play and then signal another play. The coach signals to the team that the play call is complete when he sets the play call cards down. As long as he is holding a card, he is still calling the play.

2) Another coach will signal the formation and snap count (same card). This coach will then put down the formation card and signal for the FB to block (if necessary).

3) Unless the same coach is signaling in step #2, another coach or player will signal for the FB to block.

4) A coach or player will signal the gap.

Note - I highly recommend using an additional coach or player to make the signal for the FB to block; otherwise, there will be a delay as the players wait for the coach to either signal or not signal and put down the formation card.

Changing Plays without Signaling from the Sideline

Situations will always occur when you need to make a change to a play or a receiver(s) route, but you cannot make a signal from the sideline. Make use of opportunities to do this with timeouts, changes of possession, or with a player substitution.

The team should be taught to always run toward the sideline during a timeout, even if the timeout is called by the opponent. More often than not, youth teams want to stay on the field and wait for delivery of the the water bottles, but quick sideline instruction is critical, so practice having the team head over to the coaches.

If you wish to signal a change with a player substitution, these steps should be followed:

1) The coaches should not hold up any play, formation, or gap cards.

2) The player being sent into the game should be standing in front of the primary play caller.

3) The play caller will relay the play to the player, who then repeats it back.

4) The player being sent into the field should know whom he is replacing.

5) He should sprint onto the field, after the last play is whistled dead, over to the player he is replacing, and tap him on the shoulder.

6) The player being relieved should sprint off the field.

7) The QB holds up his arms when he sees the substituted player take the field, places himself behind the ball 5 yards off the line of scrimmage, and yells, "huddle, huddle, huddle."

8) The team huddles around the QB in a circle.

9) The player coming into the game relays the new play or changes to the QB.

10) The QB repeats the instructions back to the player entering the game, and then he relays the instructions to the team twice. For example, "TE's run 10-out's, TE's run 10-out's. 21 Air Raid, 21 Air Raid."

11) The players respond with a nod of the head.

12) The QB sees this signal from all the players and then yells "Break"!

13) The team sprints to the line of scrimmage and waits for the cadence.

14) The play is then executed.

Deception

A fair amount of deception is embedded in this play-calling system already. However, to add elements that prevent other coaches from understanding your system, we put several "decoy moves" into place:

- o Have two people hold up play cards. Just let the team know which person (coach or player) is holding the actual play call. The coach could wear a black arm band or some other identifier.

- o Use a multiple of colors for the formation/snap count card background.

o Have multiple cards that have numbers, letters, words, pictures, anything, that isn't related to A, B, C, the play, formation, or snap count. Then, have another player or coach hold up those cards. They might have "45," "32," the word "Yellow" or "Orange," a picture of a basketball or any other distractors. Those cards mean nothing and the players will know it.

o Have the QB use a different cadence for each play. One play might be "Down, Set, Blue 32, Blue 32, Hut." The next play might become "Down, Set, Red 5, Red 5, Hut."

Most teams are not looking at your play-calling system. Honestly, you should hope the opposing team is trying to steal your signals. If they are spending time trying to steal your signals during the game at this level, they aren't analyzing your scheme. They are reacting to it.

I have known of situations where teams even had parents in the stands scouting another team's play-calling scheme. The scouted team still went undefeated. Regardless, you'll want a little deception because there are people who do steal signals.

The Base Offense

This chapter will be more complex than the first three because we will detail all the formations and base plays. It can almost be considered the second half of the previous chapter. You will want to fully grasp all the concepts of the base offense before proceeding into further chapters.

We will not detail how to attack every defensive front you will encounter. There are simply too many variants that a defense can provide and too many plays to make that practical in a book this size. Perhaps if there is enough interest in this material, I can write a companion to complement this book.

Also, I will not discuss much in the way of offense line blocking. Most youth line blocking schemes are very simple. What little I do discuss is described in a later chapter. There are reasons for not going into greater detail, but the most important reason is we are coaching youth football. If players and coaches had enough time and a long enough season, then I would devote a chapter to this subject. Practically speaking, you won't have enough time to go over all the complexities involved with developing a high-level offensive line scheme for every play and every defensive alignment.

In this chapter we will undertake several tasks:

o   Briefly learn how the system was developed.

o   Gain an understanding of the simple formation numbering system

o   Outline the three "base" plays that dictate the rest of the offense, with the names we call our teams: *Arkansas, Georgia,* and *LSU*

o   Learn the first passing play which we call *Air Raid.*

How the System Developed

Have you noticed the endless library of books and videos about the Wing-T offense? I'm not going to provide yet another addition to that collection. I will, however, make a few comments about how this system was developed and its relation to the Wing-T.

The Wing-T is what many coaches believe to be the best offensive football scheme that has been developed. It's a great "equalizer." That is, teams with inferior talent can be competitive against teams with better talent. They might not always win, but they will give them a run for their money.

It's a system that was developed over 40 years ago and has been detailed best in the book that is now out of print, *The Delaware Wing-T - An order of football* [2] Moreover, this book covers every nuance you could ever want about coaching the scheme. Since it is out of print and not written for youth football coaches, don't go out and pick up a copy, even if you could afford it; I've seen copies selling for hundreds of dollars online. The book's appendix lists some excellent websites that will help you understand the system.

When I started coaching, I wanted to run a system that had deception and sequences that would leave a defense guessing. I also wanted one that was relevant to the players, easy to learn, fun to play, and mostly, allow as many kids as possible to touch the football.

The first scheme that we developed was loosely based on the "Flexbone" offense, but we quickly realized its limitations. Unfortunately, in addition to its being very run-heavy, not many teams in our state were running that style of mid-line offense, and we wanted the system to be relevant for the players. The players needed to see something similar to what high schools and maybe even colleges were running.

We also wanted to have a "spread" system that made heavy use of attacking the corners rather than the midline, and the Flexbone offense didn't have those elements. But, we still wanted a good inside running game that kept defenses honest. Lastly we wanted to have a

---

[2] Raymond, H.R. "Tubby" and Ted Kempski. *The Delaware Wing-T: An Order of Football*. West Nyack: Parker Publishing Company, 1986. Print.

decent youth-style passing attack that complimented the running game.

I strongly believed that deception created by play action, motion, formation, multiple ball carriers, and multiple receiver threats was necessary, and the Wing-T offense brought those elements. So *voila*, this scheme was born.

The plays are all based on elements of the basic Wing-T offense and greatly simplified offenses of what some colleges run. I decided to quit going under the center as I wanted our quarterback to pass a little more than most teams, as well as give him and our running backs an ability to get a better look at the defense and better angles of attack. I also added the element of multiple formations that created interesting match ups and gave our offense better angles to attack defenses and disguise plays. Let's look at formations first.

Formations

The numbered, base formations we use are as follows: 10 and 1; 11; 20 and 2; 21 and 12; and 22. We also have formations specific to plays and will discuss those in a later chapter.

When you start reviewing the formations, you will notice some important and different elements to our player personnel "packages." There are no true wide-receivers (WR's). Rather, the Tight End (TE) either "slides in" and becomes a lineman or "slides out" to become a receiver (figure #1). The other aspect is additional receivers other than the TE's, in every formation, are simply the Wing Backs who "slide out."

The reason for these adaptations is speed; we don't have to substitute players. The same players stay on the field the entire offensive possession. The only time we would substitute would be to communicate a change to the scheme (e.g., blocking assignment) or to have a discussion (e.g., the player is having trouble with an element of the game).

Each formation has a purpose and your team will need to learn all of them. You will want the team to be able to switch to each formation very quickly; practice this switching with every play if at all possible.

As we go through the formations, think about your team's practice plan. I like to line up the team, switching the players back and forth between formations. I call out "10," "1," "21," "1," and etc. and see how fast they can do it without error. I give them about 8 seconds to switch and if anybody lingers too long, they must make a quick sprint to the water cooler and back.

TE and Wing Alignment

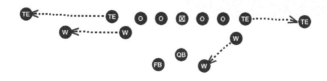

Figure #1

Lastly, a little about the system's nomenclature: a "strong-side Wing" refers to the Wing Back who is not behind the QB but just behind the offensive line or out as a receiver. The term "Wing" by itself always refers to the Wing Back who is just behind the QB.

We will start with the two most important formations in the offense. We call them "10" and "1." The name is based on the location of the TE who is used as a receiver. The formation itself looks somewhat similar to the standard "100" formation used with traditional Wing-T schemes.

Looking at the diagram of the "10" formation in figure #2, notice the numbers "1" and "0" positioned across the offense. Those are placed as a reference only and will occur in the next few formation diagrams.

o   The "1" means there is one receiver on the left side of the formation.

o   The "0" means there is no receiver on the right side of the formation.

For "10" and all formations, the formation name is based on the
number of receivers on each side of the field going left-to-right. That
is the purpose for the reference numbers in each formation figure.

"10" Formation

Figure #2

Other elements to the "10" formation and all others unless specified):

o   The left Tight End (TE), or the "1" receiver is split 6 yards
from the left Tackle (T) and remains in a 2-point stance.

o   The strong-side Wing Back (SSW) is one yard over and one
yard back off the right Tackle's right foot. He should be
aligned just to the inside of the right TE's back left hip, in a
2-point stance.

o   The Wing Back is two yards over and one yard back to the
left of the QB, in a 2-point stance.

- o The Full Back (FB) is one yard over and one yard back to the right of the QB, in a 2-point stance.

- o The QB is four (4) yards behind the Center (C).

- o Overall offensive "line splits" are two feet (24 inches) each.

- o The right TE is over 1 yard plus six (6") inches from the right Tackle (T). The right TE's will be in a three-point stance on the line as a lineman (or a two point/receiver stance when split out as a receiver).

- o All WB's (both strong-side as well as Wing) and the FB will be in the "two point" stance.

Spilts and Distances

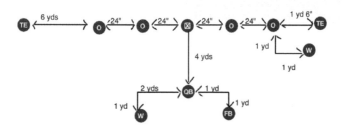

Figure #3

An illustration of the alignment can be seen in figure #3 (distances are not to scale). From this point on, the splits and spacing for all the players, in all the formations, unless specified differently, are the same as in figure #3 and as previously described.

Other formations with multiple receivers to one side or the other can require changes to the FB, TE and strong-side Wing's splits and alignment. We will describe those changes later in this chapter.

Now consider the "1" formation in figure #4. Notice it's the mirror image of the "10" formation, so no additional details are needed. The "10" and its opposite, the "1" formation, are the base formations for the entire offense.

"1" Formation

Figure #4

"11" Formation

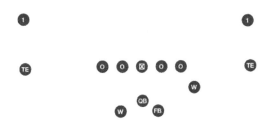

Figure #5

The Complete Offensive System for Youth Football

Figure #5 diagrams the "11" formation. This has a more balanced look about it and is our first, more obvious, three receiver formation. In "11" the position of the strong-side Wing is determined by the direction of the play call (in figure #5, the play direction would be "Red").

"21" Formation

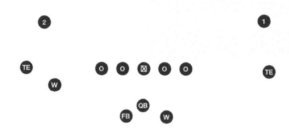

Figure #6

The next formation is "21" and is seen in figure #6. Figure #7 details the splits and distances for "21" and other formations with two (2) receivers (Wings split out to one side):

○ In the 21/12, 22, and 20/2 formations, the strong-side Wing and/or the Wing "slides out" to become a receiver.

○ The new strong-side Wing placement is six (6) yards over and one (1) yard back to the inside of the strong-side TE.

  • Note: for the TE to remain an eligible receiver, this WB must be on the inside of this TE one (1) yard back.

o The TE on the strong side of the formation (in figure #7 the "Red" side) then slides out an additional two (2) yards for a total of eight (8) yards over from the end of the offensive Tackle on his side.

"21" Alignment

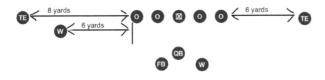

Figure #7

"12" Formation

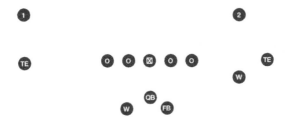

Figure #8

The Complete Offensive System for Youth Football

The "21" formation is the base formation for two plays (described in another chapter) but all plays in the scheme can be executed out of it and the mirror formation, "12." Figure #8 illustrates the "12" formation.

"20" Formation

Figure #9

"2" Formation

Figure #10

The next two formations require less discussion since they are used only in certain situations; they are called "20" and "2" and look just like "21" and "12," except the weak-side TE (in figures #9 and #10 respectively) doesn't split out.

The "22" formation appears in figure #11. This formation is generally part of the "Complex Air Raid" package of plays but can also be used for a ground attack as well.

"22" Formation

Figure #11

An important note of "22" is the location of the FB (see figure #11). You could call this formation "22 Red," which gives the FB his alignment. "22 Black" would have the FB lined up on the left side of the QB. The called play will dictate the location of the FB; however, the QB can place the FB to either side as he sees fit for pass protection if a passing play is called. The FB placement can also come from a signal for the FB to block, which I will address in another chapter.

The "22" formation looks like the typical four-receiver set and thus tends to lend itself to the passing game. Additionally, it is a good formation for a running attack and this cannot be discounted.

The Three Base Plays

Now that I have discussed the formations used in the offense, it is time to address the three base plays that dictate the entire scheme. They are called in our system "Arkansas," "Georgia," and "LSU." You will likely name them something different in your system, but my players know them as the following:

o   "Buck Sweep" – "Arkansas"

o   "Dive" – "Georgia"

o   QB "Keeper" or "Naked Boot" – "LSU"

The plays discussed in this book will be described by the names we use.

Arkansas – The Buck Sweep

The first play, "Arkansas," is a variant of the Buck Sweep used frequently as part of a Wing-T based offense. It is the only base play where offensive linemen are required to "pull" in our system.   It is highly effective at creating and setting up deception as more plays are introduced into the scheme and "combined." (Play "combining" will be explained in a later chapter.) No need to call gaps with this play as the FB dives through "A" by default. Do display a gap card, however, as a form of deception.

Running "Arkansas Black/Red" attacks the edges and opens up the middle of the field for "Georgia." The play also sets up "LSU" and later "Air Raid" as the defense starts keying on the Wing Back / FB alignment and movement.   When combined with other plays (which will be discussed later), the pulling guard action becomes a very strong key and really opens up the offense for a weak-side offensive attack.

Armed with this information, you should make this the first play your team learns to execute. They will want to master it primarily out of the "10" and "1" formations, and then move to "11," "21," and "12" formations. **This play should be learned to perfection before executing any other in the scheme.**

Figure #12 is a diagram of "10 Arkansas Red A." From this point forward, when a "mirrored" play is presented, only one half will be described as all plays are "mirrored" in the system. That is, if the text describes the "Red" play, the "Black" version of the same play operates exactly the same and vice versa, just to the other side of the field.

"10 Arkansas Red"

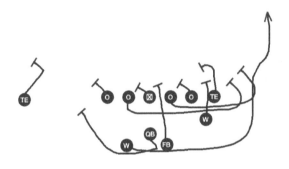

Figure #12

These steps outline the general play execution. The goal is to use the linemen and other players to form a wall, provide a lead blocker, and kick out the defensive back.

The first three steps are nearly identical for the plays "LSU," "Georgia," and "Air Raid," with the only difference being the person who receives the handoff and keeps the ball. Practice these steps until they are flawless:

1) The QB pivots 90 degrees on his right foot (he pivots 90 degrees on his left foot for "Black") and fakes a handoff to the FB.

2) The FB should "sell" that he has the ball by hunching over and learning forward as he runs through the offensive line. The FB will then break through the line and block the middle LB. If the Center isn't covered, the FB blocks the LB. If there is a defensive lineman covering the center, the LB should block him.

- Both of these potential blocks occur because the FB was directed towards the "A" gap. If the FB is assigned another gap, then the appropriate block will occur as outlined in later chapters.

- The FB should run full speed and "sell" he has the ball. This should be coached and practiced until perfect.

3) The Wing Back will turn his shoulders 90 degrees to the offensive line and start moving towards the right. At this point he should not move up the field, but be facing the sideline.

4) The QB then pivots another 90 degrees and makes one step towards the Wing Back. The two should be facing each other, with the QB just slightly not perpendicular to the offensive line. His running path as outlined in figure #12 will naturally make this happen.

5) The QB extends the ball and hands it to the Wing Back with his right hand hitting the belly of the Wing and his left hand behind the ball (opposite for "Arkansas Black").

- The hand off should not occur with the Wing facing the offensive line; he should stay facing towards the side line.

6) The Wing should have his shoulders perpendicular to the offensive line.

7) The QB's body should act as a shield so that the handoff isn't seen from the defensive side of the field; accordingly, he remains tilted slightly towards the backfield as he continues in an arcing path.

8) The Wing Back now has the football and continues running toward the right side of the field.

9) The Wing Back should be looking for the two pulling guards and follow them around the end of the line.

   • The left Guard will block the first inside defender he encounters. The right Guard will be used as a lead blocker or a "kick out." Most youth teams will leave the CB on an island alone when they see the "10" or "1" formation; therefore, unlike the typical Buck Sweep, there may be no man to kick out. The play diagram in figure #12 makes this assumption.

   • Many youth Wing Backs have a tendency to out run their pulling guards. That is, they make it to the end of the offensive line before the guards get there. They should be patient and not do this; they should learn to follow their blockers. Coach this until you see a perfect execution.

10) The right pulling guard should be sealing off the next defensive player to the inside, usually a linebacker (LB), if there is no CB to kick out. That is, he will pick up the CB and either push him right towards the side line, or seal him inside if he is aligned inside.

11) The QB continues to act as if he still has the football and runs, full speed, the route outlined in the diagram until the whistle has blown the play dead. For "LSU" and "Air Raid," the QB will keep the ball, so this fake is highly important.

- The QB should run full speed and "sell" he has the ball until the whistle is blown. Coach and practice until perfectly performed.

12) The offensive line should be "blocking down" to their left.

13) The strong-side TE, out of the "10" formation, does not block the defensive end (DE), if there is one on him to block. He should leave him alone, peal off, and block the outside LB.

14) The strong-side Wing should then block the DE and seal him inside.

15) The Wing Back with the ball should look for the "wall" and run towards the end of the offensive line, turn his shoulders up field, and run towards the hash mark and then the side-line.

The action between the WB, QB, and FB in steps #1 - #8 should be practiced to perfection. The action creates deception with the defense, slowing their attack and becomes necessary for the entire offense to be successful. The action also creates the potential for 3 ball carriers, a principle of the Wing-T offense. This potential exists in nearly all plays in the scheme and is the key for success.

Georgia – Dive

"Georgia" is the second base play to the offensive scheme. We will introduce gaps with this play. In figure #13 we see "10 Georgia Red A" illustrated.

The action of this play among the QB, FB, and WB is exactly the same as outlined in "Arkansas," except the QB will hand the ball off to the FB. See the reference below:

1. The QB pivots 90 degrees on his right foot (he pivots 90 degrees on his left foot for "Black") and hands the ball off to

the FB. The FB will then continue a route towards and through the gap card held up by the team. In most cases this will be the A, B, and then the C gaps in that order depending on the defensive alignment.

"10 Georgia Red"

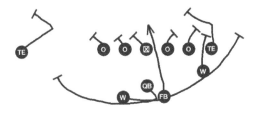

Figure #13

2. The Wing Back will turn his shoulders 90 degrees to the offensive line and start moving towards the right. At this point he should not move up the field.

3. The QB then pivots another 90 degrees and makes one step towards the Wing Back. The two should be facing each other, with the QB just slightly but not perpendicular to the offensive line. His running path as outlined above will naturally make this happen.

4. The QB extends the ball and fakes a handoff to the Wing Back with his right hand hitting the belly of the Wing and his left hand behind the ball (opposite for Arkansas Black).

5. The Wing Back should "sell" that he has the football by hunching over slightly and running, full speed, as if he's going to go around the TE.

- Note: The Wing should run full speed and "sell" he has the ball until the whistle is blown. This should be coached and practiced until perfect.

6. The QB continues to act as if he still has the football and runs, full speed, the route outlined in the diagram until the whistle has blown the play dead.

- Note: The QB should run full speed and "sell" he has the ball until the whistle is blown. This should be coached and practiced until perfect.

There are no pulling guards when this play is executed as a base play. It can be combined with other plays (which will be discussed in a later chapter) which make this a very effective play.

LSU – Quarterback Keep

The last base play looks identical in almost every aspect to "Georgia" except the ball carrier is the QB and the offensive line blocks down to the play call side. That is, if the play is "LSU Black," then the offensive line blocks to the Red side; if the play is "LSU Red," the line blocks to the Black side. Figure #14 diagrams the play "10 LSU Black."

The action between the FB and Wing Back is exactly the same, except each player hunches over and fakes that he is the ball carrier. The FB and Wing must run their routes at full speed and sell they have the ball. Lastly, the guards do not pull, although that can again be an aspect when combined with other plays (which will be detailed in a later chapter).

1) The QB pivots 90 degrees on his right foot (he pivots 90 degrees on his left foot for "Black") and fakes a handoff to the FB.

2) The FB should "sell" that he has the ball by hunching over and learning forward as he runs through the offensive line.

3) The Wing Back will turn his shoulders 90 degrees to the offensive line and start moving towards the right. At this point he should not move up the field.

4) The QB then pivots another 90 degrees and makes one step towards the Wing Back. The two should be facing each other, with the QB just slightly but not perpendicular to the offensive line. His running path as outlined above will naturally make this happen.

5) The QB extends the ball and fakes the handoff to the Wing Back with his right hand hitting the belly of the Wing and his left hand behind the ball.

6) The Wing Back should "sell" that he has the football by hunching over slightly and running, full speed, as if he's going to go around the TE.

"10 LSU Black"

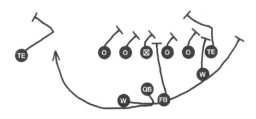

Figure #14

7) The QB runs the route as outlined in Figure #14.

The QB does not need to roll opposite the play action. He can fake the handoff to the Wing and then follow him along his route. The Wing will need to change his role and become a blocker; realignment of the FB is also highly suggested. This aspect will be described in a later chapter.

This play is extremely effective if it's not run for a couple of series. That is, it shouldn't be called until you've run "Arkansas Red/Black," "Georgia Red/Black," and a few times each.

This play also perfectly sets up the primary passing play called "Air Raid." A combination of the two (LSU/Air Raid) will really get the defense guessing. You'll want to run "LSU" at least twice before transitioning to "Air Raid," which is described next.

The Passing Game

While there isn't much passing in this system, but what passing there is becomes critical to the success of the entire offense. The passing game adds another element of deception and uncertainty in the minds of the defensive players and coaches and will lead to overall offensive success. Your team will want to become proficient in execution.

Air Raid

A primary principle in a Wing-T offense is that of three potential ball carriers. There is also another principle of a 3-deep passing threat on every play, and you will notice that every formation has at least three potential receivers. Keep this principle in mind as we discuss the next play in figure #16 or "Air Raid."

The play name "Air Raid" is self-explanatory and is consistent with the play-naming rules I have already discussed. While it is our first pass play, it could almost be considered one of the "base" plays of the offense. You will definitely want this play installed by your first game.

You will want to select a play name and picture as outlined earlier in the book for use in your system and on the play-calling card. Figure #15 illustrates the picture we use.

Once you have established your picture, you do not need to consider border or background color. The play direction is dictated by formation and how it is combined with other plays (this aspect of the offense will be detailed in a later chapter).

Figure #15

Figure #16 is the play diagram for "Air Raid." Note the similarity to "LSU" and this play:

"10 Air Raid"

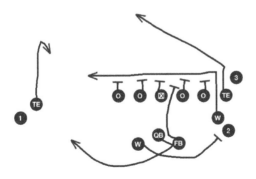

Figure #16

1) The action between the QB, FB and WB will be exactly the same as in "LSU" except the FB and WB will both receive fake handoffs and block the QB's back to the strong-side of the play.

   • The "strong-side" for the "10" formation is the "Red" side of the field; for the "1" formation it is the "Black".

2) The weak-side TE will run a 10 yard "curl-in" route.

3) The weak-side TE becomes the primary receiver (labeled #1).

4) The strong-side Wing becomes the secondary receiver (labeled #2). This receiver will run a short 5-yard "in" route.

5) The strong-side TE becomes the 3rd potential receiver (labeled #3). This receiver will run a 5-yard "post" (shown) or a 5-yard "out" route (not shown). The choice of route depends on coaches' preferences based on defensive alignment.

6) The offensive linemen should remember two major points:

   • Never block beyond 2-yards from the line-of-scrimmage down field; if they do, they will become ineligible receivers.

   • Remain in the 3-point stance on the line.

7) The FB and Wing continue to run their routes except in the case of protecting the QB's blind side. If a LB or defensive lineman breaks through the line, he should block that man after he has received the fake handoff.

8) If the TE is not open, the QB should "tuck and run" and treat the play as he would "LSU."

   The play action for "Air Raid" is determined by formation and play-call combination (which will be discussed in a later chapter). In this case, the formation "10" indicates that the QB will be rolling to his left or the "Black" side of the field. The primary receiver will be the TE.

A key component to this play and the entire offense in general – the primary receiver will always be the TE, regardless of the formation and which side the QB rolls.

Perfect execution is the most important aspect of "Air Raid." Since we only pass a few times a game, we want to be very successful every time we do it. Fortunately, this play is usually a success, regardless how late in the season it is executed. Most youth teams simply don't have the discipline to stay with the receiver after they have seen "LSU" run a few times a game. But success only comes with excellent execution. That is the primary reason for using the same pass routes, same primary receiver, same personnel, and same play action.

This play is also effective out of a number of formations. Because of this, you will want to give the "10" or "1" formation look once or twice, and then run it out of the "11," "12," or "21" formation. Note, however, when you change the formation from "10" or "1," you should consider "combining" "Air Raid" with another play to give the QB directions as to which TE becomes the primary receiver. I will detail "play combining" in another chapter as there are several considerations when making this decision.

With "Air Raid," the choices of pass routes for the receivers, at least for the first three games, are static; they are pre-determined and do not change. Later in the season you can change those routes, but the routes for each game will remain the same unless changed ingame. If you believe by the third game that the opponent is familiar with your pass routes, feel free to introduce changes as outlined in another chapter.

We do not use a "Route Tree" which is typical in a HUNH and similar offensive systems. I believe the additional complexity required communicating and practicing the use of a Route Tree (and multiple pass routes) outweighs any benefit to a youth, heavily run-oriented team. This extra complexity is especially not needed for a team that doesn't pass a great deal.

We set the TE as the primary receiver for simplicity. The QB doesn't have to make a read and decide on the best receiver. This doesn't mean that the QB cannot choose another receiver. While at the youth level, the QB always keying on the TE takes pressure off his having to make a decision.

Starting with the second full practice, the TE's, Wings, and the FB on each side of the formation will learn these routes:

- o TE's –
    - o 10-yard "Curl" (both in and out),
    - o 5-yard "Post",
    - o 10-Yard "Post"
    - o 5-yard "In" and "Out"
    - o 10-yard "In" and "Out"
- o Wings –
    - o 5-yard "In" and "Out"
    - o "Wheel"
    - o 5-yard "Curl" (both in and out)
- o FB – 5-yard "Curl" (both in and out)

While not all of these routes are used until later in the season, the players will want to become familiar with them as early as possible. The Curl, Post, and In routes are the most important for the first pass play, so extra emphasis should be added at the second and third practices. If more practices are available before your first game, you should still continue to work on these routes and add the other routes only after your first game.

The TE's should almost always run a 10-yard route. Because of the play action nature of the offense, they need time to get open. The QB must generally execute fake handoffs and then roll out. This requires some time and a 10-yard route allows the needed time. If you chose to use a 5-yard route for the TE's, consider a "max protect" package (which will be described later) that has essentially no play action.

You will decide which routes to use before the game and communicate them to the team. If you need to change routes in-game, the play-call system doesn't have a means to do this, but they can be changed as outlined in the previous chapter (i.e., time out, substitution, or change of possession and etc.).

Final Thoughts about the Scheme Design

Believers who are focused on a "Power-I" scheme as well as those who are Wing-T enthusiasts are something akin to cults. Honestly, there's nothing wrong with the Power-I in youth football. The line blocking schemes are very similar to the Wing-T; however, the Power-I relies on the team having a really good tailback; they simply toss it to him. While there's usually a team or two who will have a really great TB, most do not have this luxury. In addition, only one or two guys will generally get a chance to carry the football when running out of the Power-I. Our scheme allows several kids to touch the ball (three and sometimes even four potential ball carriers and at least another three potential receivers). Combined with the better blocking angles from formation alignment, I believe you will have greater success without the need for an All-Star TB in our Wing-T based scheme.

This offense is designed as a much-simpler version of a type of Wing-T. The three base plays, "Air Raid," and all of the formations utilize some of the core principals of the Wing-T offense:

o   The potential of at least 3 different ball carriers
o   The potential of a 3-deep passing threat.
o   An attack of the flanks.
o   The use of the play-action to set up the pass.

While there are seemingly multiple ways to attack a defense, in reality there are only three: the gut, off-tackle, and the flank. Each base play was designed with these three attacks in mind.

In the next chapter, I will take a brief pause and not go over plays but the FB position and how he should be utilized to make the base plays more effective. In the chapter "Added Offensive Complexity," I will give you more weapons to attack the three key fronts, building on the base plays and strengthening the offense.

The Full Back

In a previous chapter I discussed how to communicate to the offense when and where the FB should block. Up until this point, I haven't discussed this position in any great detail. In this chapter I will explore the FB position because his role adds needed offensive complexity. This complexity is critical as you build the scheme and add more plays.

A principle of this scheme is that the FB is the premier back in this offense. By "premier" I mean he is key to successful execution because of how he is utilized. Hence, when choosing a player for FB, these characteristics should be considered:

- o He doesn't have to be the fastest runner (your WB's should be the fastest), but he needs to be smart, strong, and willing to block.

- o He will be a ball carrier, but more often than not he will not score many touchdowns; therefore, he should be unselfish and a true team player.

- o He should be excellent at "receiving" a fake handoff as deception is critical.

FB Blocking

In all plays in which the FB receives a fake handoff, he will block through the gap or as otherwise communicated. His blocking assignment is determined as follows:

1) If the signal is given for the FB to block, he will always be a lead blocker for the primary ball carrier. He will block either through his assigned gap, or he will block for the primary ball carrier's expected route.

2) If the play is one in which the action is to attack the flank and the FB is not given a signal to block, he will receive his fake

handoff and block either through the assigned gap, or he will block to the primary ball carrier's "blind side" as appropriate.

There are two different modes to utilize the FB to block in this offense as outlined above. As the coach, you will decide based on your team's ability to learn these modes:

Mode 1: requires nothing of the FB other than to block where directed and as outlined above based on the play call.

Mode 2: requires the FB to realign his position in the formation when signaled to block.

Don't feel pressure to ask very young teams (under 9 year olds) to have the FB realigned (when assigned to block) due to the added complexity. When realigned, the FB will need to understand when he can and can't motion based on the play and that requires a little more comprehension of the system (more on this later in the chapter).

The first mode of the scheme requires no changes to the FB alignment. You will simply call a play and signal the FB to block.

Thinking about the Mode 1, having the FB simply block, we first review figure #1. In this figure the FB is being used to block in the play "10 Arkansas Red FB Red." The only difference between "10 Arkansas Red" and "10 Arkansas Red FB Red" is the QB does not fake to the FB in the later, rather the execution goes like this:

1) The QB will pivot 180 degrees and step with no fake handoff to the FB.

2) The QB then performs a handoff to the Wing and continues on his route, using the same play action as "LSU."

3) The FB will then act as another blocker for the Wing; sealing the defender to the inside and helping creating a wall and lane for the Wing's route.

10 Arkansas Red FB Block Red

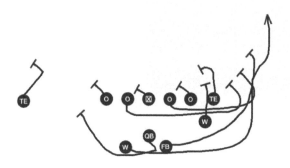

Figure #1

Now consider Mode 2 which requires *realignment* of the FB in the formation as shown in figure #2. He will align himself, when signaled to block, to either the "Red" or "Black" side of the field by placing himself two (2) yards behind the offensive Tackle. For example, if he is signaled to block to the "Red" side, he will place himself 2 yards directly behind the tackle to the right side of the offensive line. Figure #2 shows the new FB alignment using the "10" formation, with a "Red" play call and the FB signaled to align to that side. For simplicity, other splits and distances are not detailed in the diagram as they don't change.

Let's consider the FB alignment and blocking assignment using the play "10 Arkansas Red FB Red" in figure #3. In this alignment, the FB will have a better blocking angle and be well ahead of the ball carrier (as little as 5 yards if not more): a position he would otherwise not have if he was aligned in the standard "10" formation and simply lead blocking.

In figure #4 we see "10 LSU Black FB Black" with the FB aligned to the "Black" side of the field behind the left Tackle. The QB will now have a lead blocker in the FB.

The FB should be coached to recognize this principle of his position - he is always blocking for the primary ball carrier when signaled to block.

Splits - FB Red

Figure #2

10 Arkansas Red - FB Red

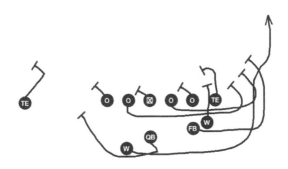

Figure #3

10 LSU Black - FB Black

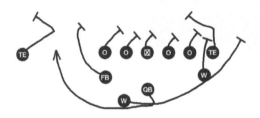

Figure #4

Last, let's look at the "21" formation with the FB aligned behind the offensive Tackle to the "Black" side of the formation in figure #5. This formation becomes stronger to that side when using the FB in this alignment than it would otherwise have been.

The advantages of moving the FB have been discussed. Primarily realignment gains a blocking advantage; moreover, additional to that gain, there is the element of changing tendencies. If you work realignment of the FB into your team's scheme, you add another look that will throw off defenses.

There are two disadvantages to realignment:

o   It can be a key for the defense as to the side of the field the play is expected to go.

o   You lose a potential ball carrier and the deception that is gained using him for of a fake handoff.

Therefore, as a coach, you will need to consider and weigh the gains and losses from realignment. I believe when executed properly, at the right time and with the right conditions, moving the FB has more advantages than disadvantages.

"21" - FB Black

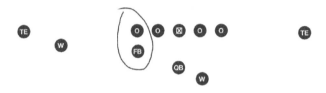

Figure #5

Adding FB Motion

The last aspect to having the FB change his alignment is the introduction of motion. This brings another level of complexity that very young teams might have a hard time grasping; as the coach, you will need to determine if your team can handle the added complexity.

FB motion is introduced when he is realigned opposite of the play direction with or without a "combined" play (which will be described in a later chapter). FB motion works like this:

o The FB is aligned to the opposite side of the field where the primary play action will occur.

o The FB then motions and changes his alignment at the proper time in the QB's cadence.

Let's review two examples of FB motion using the base plays "10 Arkansas Red FB Black" and "10 LSU Black FB Red" as seen in figures #6 and #7. In both plays the FB is signaled to block, but he blocks opposite the primary play action. Therefore, the FB will know that he should go into motion at the proper time in the QB's cadence because of this contradiction (his alignment versus the play's primary direction).

10 Arkansas Red - FB Black

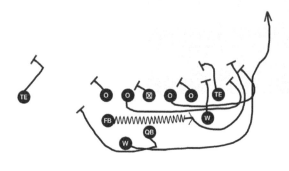

Figure #6

10 LSU Black - FB Red

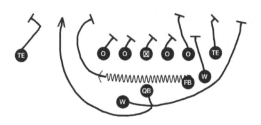

Figure #7

There are two types of motion the FB can make:

1) The FB is facing the offensive line, turns his shoulders perpendicular to the line and starts his motion. This motion is used for all plays except as outlined in the next step.

2) The FB continues facing the offensive line and side-steps with his shoulders square to the line. This type of motion is used only when a "variant" play is called, such as "Georgia Bob," where he is a lead blocker through the required gaps, A, B, and etc. (which will be explained in the another chapter). This is also highly complex and not required for young team (under 12 years of age).

The QB must change his cadence to account for the FB crossing behind the center. Therefore, you will need to install additional drills to help the QB, FB and offensive Center anticipate and adjust for the motion. This is not difficult to teach but must be practiced to assure on-field success.

The FB will need to understand when he is to motion and when he is not. The rules are simple but need to be practiced:

1) The offense has realigned the FB (a decision the coach makes)

2) The FB is signaled to block and aligns himself to this instruction based on his signaled alignment or the FIRST play called when plays are "combined" (explained in a later chapter).

3) The second play is signaled or step #4

4) The QB starts his cadence, "Down, set" and the FB begins his motion

5) Once the FB has crossed the line behind the center to the QB, the QB finishes his cadence and says, "Hut!"

Note: The FB should never motion if the called play requires any Wing Back to go into pre-snap motion.

The introduction of motion to the FB position adds complexity but gains some advantages:

- o The defense sees another element of complexity and this can create poor decision-making on their part.

- o The FB in motion, when the play is snapped, gives him a momentum advantage when making a block.

- o The FB motion can allow the coach to better break apart of the defense and reveal the defenses coverage. In a youth defense this is rarely a consideration, but it can happen,

Using figure #8 as an example, you will see motion introduced using a "combined" play "10 Arkansas Red LSU Black FB Red." In figure #8, he is aligned "Red," but the play action will go to the 'Black' side of the field. In this example the play is combined with another play and the FB aligns to the first play called. Keep this principle in mind when I go into further detail about this aspect of the offense in later chapter.

10 Arkansas Red LSU Black FB Red

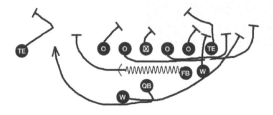

Figure #8

We have discussed the use of the FB and how this position is critical to the execution of the offense. We have explored how to use him to block in two different ways. Lastly, we have seen how to employ the FB as part of a motion package. In the next chapter I will introduce additional but more complex plays which require further use of an effective FB.

Added Offensive Complexity

The first four plays the team should learn to execute perfectly are the Buck Sweep ("Arkansas), the Dive ("Georgia"), QB Keep ("LSU"), and a Waggle Pass ("Air Raid"). These plays should be learned as previously diagrammed and explained, out of the "10" and "1" formations initially.

Once your team has mastered these plays, you will then add some complexity by changing the formations to "21" and "12." You should practice switching back and forth very quickly.

Lastly, you should introduce the use of the FB as a blocker. Whether the FB realigns or not is up to you; however, the offense should learn this important element of the system.

Until this point the plays are rather simple and should not put the players into any situation where interpretation of the play-call is difficult. That fact is going to change as you add new elements to your offense.

In this chapter we will learn how to increase the complexity of the offense:

o   Add new and more complex plays with Jet and FB motion –
     Jet Sweep, Jet Dive, Speed Option ("Auburn") and Fake
     Reverse ("Oregon")

o   Expanded plays using variations (a "Sponge Bob" play)

We have discussed the formations, base plays, and our first passing play. We have also discussed FB realignment and motion. At this point your team actually has quite an arsenal considering the multiple looks available from each formation, play, and FB alignment. However, each of the plays will become less effective as the team gets deeper into the season. Because of the reduced effectiveness, a new set of plays and looks should be introduced by game #4 (at the latest) and as early as game #3 if at all possible.

Your team should be executing the base offense with perfection before introduction of these series of plays. They require motion, timing, and the ability to "option" the football, adding yet more complexity to the offense. In addition, we will introduce further modifications to the base plays that add yet another element of complexity, so perfect execution is a must. We call these special variants of the base plays or simply "Bob" in our system. The name will be explained later.

The Jet Series

The next two plays use what is known as "Jet Motion." The plays are called "Jet Red/Black" and "Jet Dive Red/Black"; since the play names fit the naming rules we outlined in an earlier chapter, we simply use those names as other teams might.

The pre-snap motion is typically run out of the "21" and "12" formations, but it will work out of all of them. In addition, while Jet Red/Black is a play, it is also used as a motion package that can be combined with other plays (as explained later).

While the Wings are used to block in the offense and size is important, their overall speed is the most important aspect. The Wings typically attack the flanks, and the Jet Sweep does this with effectiveness. In figure #6 we see the play diagrammed as "12 Jet Black."

12 Jet Black

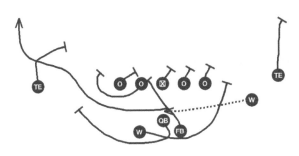

Figure #6

The play execution works as follows:
1) The QB calls out "Down, Set"

2) When "Set" is called, the strong-side Wing goes in to full-speed motion, almost sprinting, moving in a 3-yard arc towards the front of the QB (as you recall, he is set one yard back from the offensive line).

3) While the motion is occurring, the QB will continue his cadence. Something like, "Red 32, Red 32;" whatever you decide is fine.

4) When the strong-side Wing is 1 yard away, the QB calls "Hut."

5) The QB does not move, but he executes a handoff to the strong-side Wing as he passes in front of him.

6) The QB then begins the same series of actions he would execute as in "Arkansas," "Georgia," and "LSU." He will pivot on his right foot (left foot for Jet Red), fake handoffs to the FB, then to the Wing, then he will start his route like he's running "LSU." The FB blocking for the pulling guard, will dive through the A-gap.

7) The left (e.g., "Black") side guard will pull in the direction of the ball carrier and block the first man who comes off the edge.

8) The TE to the action side will block his man to the inside.

9) The strong-side Wing (ball carrier) will then run a route as defined by the "Hash, Numbers, and Side Line." That is, he will aim for the hash mark, the field numbers, and then the side line.

The timing of this play is absolutely critical or several things can happen that will ruin it. Practice requires going over the QB cadence and handoff repeatedly. Do not neglect to have the QB continue the action to the FB and Wing.

As we learned in an earlier chapter, we can realign the FB so he is behind the offensive Tackle to the play side. The Jet Sweep series is a prime candidate to make this happen. Figure #7 diagrams the realignment using "21 Jet Red." You can run this play out of all formations and combine with other plays (I will describe in a later chapter) and produce maneuvers that will confuse young defenses.

21 Jet Red FB Red

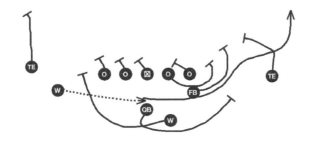

Figure #7

22 Jet Black

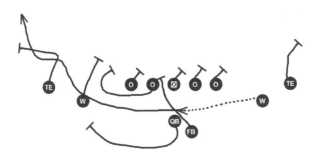

Figure #8

11 Jet Red (Black formation)

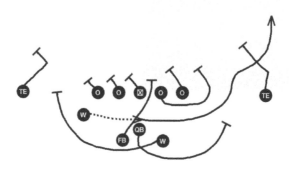

Figure #9

Figures #8 and #9 provide the diagrams of how to run the Jet sweep out of two other formations, "22" and "11" respectively. While "22" is traditionally a passing set, "Jet Sweep" or "Jet Dive" is also effective.

The next play that is part of the Jet Series is called "Jet Dive" and is a simple variant to the "Jet Sweep" play. Figure #10 illustrates the play diagram "21 Jet Red Dive A."

In "Jet Dive," there are some differences as compared to the "Jet Sweep" play:

1) The guard does not pull to the play side.
2) The QB fakes a handoff to the strong-side Wing in "Jet" motion, pivots 90 degrees to his left (for a Black play), and hands the ball off to the FB.

The FB will be given a gap designation which is generally opposite the play side as this prevents a collision of the players. That is, if the play is "Jet Red Dive," the FB will be given a gap on the "Black" side of the play. For example, in figure #10 the play's motion is "Jet Red" and the FB will be diving to the "A" gap on the "Black" side of the field. There is no method to signal this change in our play call system, so the change would be communicated as described in a previous chapter.

21 Jet Red Dive

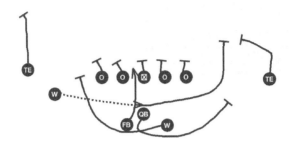

Figure #10

The Speed Option and Fake Reverse

The next two plays are the final two running plays in the scheme. While the plays are executed out of the "21" formation (or "12"), the location of the FB changes in the "Speed Option," which is the play we call "Auburn." The other play is a "Fake Reverse" which we call "Oregon" and the FB is not aligned differently.

Figure #11 diagrams "Auburn" and is executed as follows:

1) The FB is placed in the "21" formation where the strong-side Wing would ordinarily be.

2) The QB starts his cadence, "Down, Set" and then the FB goes into a slow motion towards the opposite side of the field (in figure #11 he will motion towards the "Red" side). The motion is slow as he will only need to go a couple of yards before the QB says "hut."

3) The QB finishes his cadence, "Blue 21, Blue 21, Hut!"

4) The FB will then take one step as if he's headed to the backfield, and then he heads downfield in the route shown in figure #11. I call it a "sloppy 3-yard in."

5) The FB will then seal to the inside and block the first defensive player he encounters as he is facing the red side of the

field. This is usually the outside LB. He is not to block any players to his back or left.

6) The QB will fake a handoff to the strong-side Wing that is now in the FB position.

7) The Wing and QB will proceed on the routes identified in figure #11. The Wing will start lined up 2 yards behind the QB and his route will take him to no closer than 1 yard to the QB's left or right arm (depending on the play direction - in this example to his left).

8) At the first encounter with a defensive player, the QB will make the decision to either hold on to the football, or pitch it to the Wing who is mirroring him on his left (or right if the play goes to the "Red" side). If the Wing is covered, the QB should hang on to the football and run forward.

"21 Auburn Black"

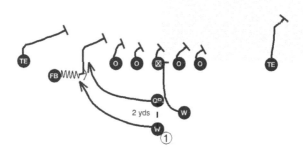

Figure #11

This is an excellent play when it's first executed to make the defense loosen up in the middle of the field, which opens up "Georgia," "Georgia Bob," (which will be described later) and "Jet Dive." The additional motion and placement of the FB also creates a new and unexpected twist. The exchange of the FB for the strong-side Wing is made primarily to provide an additional blocker. This exchange also creates confusion for the defense.

The "pitch" action between the QB and Wing should be practiced until perfect. It will need to be practiced going both left and right and with each Wing to that side respectively.

The timing of the pitch is critical and location of the Wing receiving the pitch is just as important. The Wing must stay directly beside the QB, and the pitch cannot be behind but to his side. These elements are what make this a more difficult play to master but worth the effort.

Another play that is similar to "Auburn" is the fake reverse which we call "Oregon." This play takes the action of "Auburn" and adds another element, creating a fake reverse. Before continuing further, a point should be made that I generally do not like "trick" plays and don't believe they are necessary for overall success. However, there are rare occasions when they can be used (which I will discuss later). I do not consider "Oregon" a "trick" play. It is a staple of the system and is executed a couple of times per game.

Figure # 12 diagrams this play:

"21 Oregon Black"

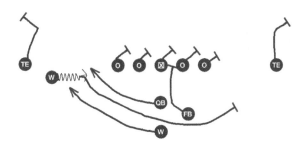

Figure #12

Most youth coaches are very tempted to run a true reverse. Quite frankly, the reverse is generally only effective with the youngest of teams. While they can be successful, it is used in our scheme very sparingly; generally, the fake reverse is most effective at slowing defenses. Combining "Oregon" with an option element makes for a very powerful attack.

The play is executed like "Auburn" with some exceptions:

1) The FB is back in his regular placement in the 21 (or 12) formation.
2) The QB pivots 90 degrees and fakes a handoff to the FB.
3) The QB then pivots another 180 degrees, almost facing the defense directly but heading in an arc towards the field hash mark.
4) While the QB is running his route, to his left (when running to the black side) the strong-side Wing will be coming back across the formation as outlined in figure #12, between the QB and the Wing.
5) The QB then fakes a handoff, while running, to the strong-side Wing who is coming back across the formation. The QB will extend his hands and allow the ball to almost touch the belly of the Strong-Side Wing, but he retracts the ball after they pass.
6) The QB may then, if needed, use the Wing to his left (or right as appropriate), as a potential "option man."

Note: The Strong Side Wing should always pass between the QB and the Wing. The reason for this is that the fake handoff between the QB and Strong Side Wing is disguised; it can't be clearly seen. The defense can't see if an exchange is made, so they must wait and look for the ball carrier. The Strong-Side Wing should "sell" he has the ball and run full speed on his route.

You will need to practice the fake handoff to the Strong-Side Wing at full speed, as timing is critical. The QB action faking to the FB is equally critical and should not be neglected when practicing the play.

Variants to Plays

In the system are a few plays which have "variations" that are not part of "combining plays," which we will discuss in the next chapter. Variations to existing plays allow you to change tendencies that the defense will need to adjust. We won't detail all of the variants that are possible or all the ones that we use; we'll leave that up to your imagination. Rather, we will focus on just one play, "Georgia" or the "Dive."

We call variants to a play using a special signal from the play call card. We use a signal, a picture called "Sponge Bob." When the players see a called play with Sponge Bob, they know it's different. To make the signal the coach will hold one hand on "Sponge Bob" and one hand on "Georgia" (or your play(s) with a variant). This signals "Georgia Bob."

We chose Sponge Bob because the kids remember him easily and know this about him – there is something "not quite right" about Sponge Bob Square Pants. You can choose any naming convention and picture you want; just remember that the name and picture should send the same signal – something is different about the play.

Figure #13 illustrates the use of Sponge Bob:

Figure #13

A few plays use Sponge Bob in our scheme, but you will easily see he can be adapted to others. It's up to you to decide how many, (if any) you'll want to implement, but I suggest no more than three (3) to four (4). Too many variants and the kids might get confused.

Looking at "Georgia Bob" in figure #14, you will see that the primary ball carrier is no longer the FB but the WB. When implementing a play with a variant, you should consider changes in the primary action of the QB, FB, and WB. If there are changes to this action, be sure to incorporate them into your practice plans.

The play "Georgia Bob" now has a much more traditional off-tackle power look as the WB is the ball carrier and the FB is the blocker, attacking the C gap. Other examples of "Georgia Bob" are seen in figures #15 and #16.

You will note in figure #16 that while the action is off tackle and the TE is split out to that side, the route is still considered the "C" gap in our system. You will want to point this out to your team to prevent any confusion.

10 Georgia Red Bob C

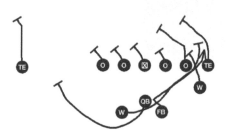

Figure #14

12 Georgia Red Bob B

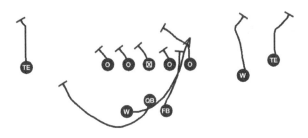

Figure #15

11 Georgia Black Bob C

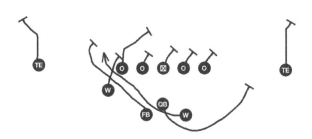

Figure #16

There are other potential variants that can be added. Here are a couple of ideas:

1) "Auburn Bob" – the Wing placed in the FB position actually receives the handoff and executes a "dive" or "Georgia."
2) "Oregon Bob" – the FB actually receives the handoff and executes a "dive" or "Georgia."

At this point your offense has a good stock of plays and formations, with the potential for more looks as you can create and communicate variants for each play. The next chapter will detail how you can create more complex plays that will really confound defenses.

Opening up the Offense by Combining Plays

A powerful aspect of this offense is the ability to create complex plays that make the scheme appear more multi-faceted and complicated and prevents the defense from making "keys". We call it "Play Combining." No new plays are actually introduced, but the existing plays are combined with other established plays, creating entirely new looks. You will find that your team can likely adopt every combination you can throw at them. Some of these combinations will necessitate changes to the QB, FB, and Wing actions, but this can be coached and practiced quite easily.

You can introduce this creativity in your play calling very early in the season, as soon as the second game. The kids really enjoy the changes, and as a coach, you will enjoy calling the plays. More importantly, combined plays produce a better overall offense.

The system works as it sounds. The coach will call a play, then another play (then the formation, gap and FB blocking requirement as appropriate). The second play called is the key to the offense as to the actual play action. That is, the primary ball carrier, ball carrier's route, play action, or passing action.

For example, the coach calls the combined play "10 Arkansas Red LSU Black." The play works like this:

- o The coach will hold up the play calling card with his hand on "Arkansas Red."
- o The coach will then hold up a play calling card with his hand on "LSU Black."
- o Another coach or player will then hold up the formation card touching the "10."
- o Another coach or player will hold up the "A, B, or C" gap card.
- o The offensive line, Wing, and FB then execute "Arkansas Red." However, the QB will not hand the ball off to the Wing, but he will fake the handoff and execute "LSU Black."

Using this example, play action will seem to go to the Red side of the field, with the guards pulling exactly as if the play is "Arkansas." However, rather than the QB handing the ball off to the Wing, the QB will keep it and run "LSU" to the Black side of the field. You will note that this combination play does not require changes to the Wing or FB movement or offensive line blocking.

The action is very powerful because, in every aspect, the play looks exactly like "Arkansas Red." As you remember, "LSU" and "Georgia" do not require any pulling guards or changes to the offensive line blocking assignment. Therefore, defenses will start noting that the guards pull for only "Arkansas." If your team executes "Arkansas Red" combined with "LSU Black," the defense will have only seen offensive guards pulling to the play direction and will key off of that. Figure #1 outlines the play:

10 Arkansas Red LSU Black

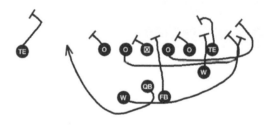

Figure #1

The play "Air Raid" can also be combined with any other play presented out of any formation. For example, in figure #2, we see the play diagram "21 Arkansas Black Air Raid FB Red." The play action looks very similar to "Arkansas Black." The guards will pull and go to the Black side and the Wing fakes as if he has the ball and continues to the same side. However, the QB will run his route and then stop and pass as he does for a standard "Air Raid" play. Please note that while the guards pull, they cannot proceed downfield to block or they will become ineligible receivers.

21 Arkansas Black Air Raid FB Red

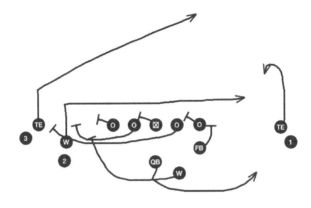

Figure #2

The pulling guards' actions combined with the moves in "Air Raid" can really throw off a defense and make this an especially effective play. It will flummox defenses and keep them guessing.

You can also notice in figure #2 that the FB has also been directed to realign to block to the Red side of the offensive line. This alignment allows the FB to block the QB's most vulnerable side. If you recall, you can also align the FB to the Black side and he will motion to the Red. The FB could also become a potential receiver. Since the offense doesn't have a means to communicate this change with the standard play calling system, you will need to communicate this change at a time-out, possession change, or etc.

Consider inherent advantages and disadvantages to each combined play. You will want to study and determine appropriateness based on your team's abilities and what the opposing defenses present.

The following figures show samplings of potential ways that plays can be combined. I think you'll find that in most cases the players will execute them, even if they are unpracticed. You will still need to regularly practice combined plays, but throw in something different to test reactions.

The Complete Offensive System for Youth Football

12 Auburn Air Raid

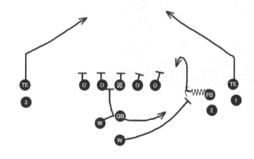

Figure #3

12 Jet Black LSU Red FB Red

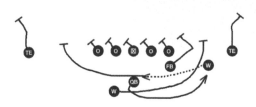

Figure #4

Note – there is a change in the primary QB action in figure #4.

Pat Moss

21 Georgia Red LSU Black

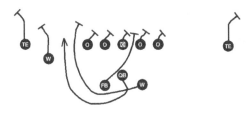

Figure #5

21 Georgia Red C LSU Black FB Red

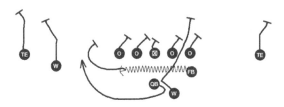

Figure #6

Note - there is a change in the primary QB action in figures #5 and #6. "21 GA Red LSU Black FB Red" is especially complex as the QB's pivot is opposite the typical play action.

12 Jet Black Arkansas Red FB Red

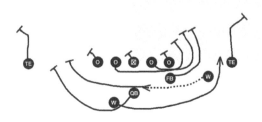

Figure #7

Note - there is a change in the primary QB action in figure #7.

Some plays don't make sense to combine: the result is simply a base or an existing play. For example, there's no need to call "10 Georgia Red LSU Black," since "10 LSU Black" is the same play. In addition, no plays should be combined with "Georgia" or "Jet Dive" as the *second* play, since the play action already exists (e.g., part of the primary play action) unless the the "Bob" signal is given (e.g., "Georgia Bob").

Lastly, when developing combined plays, consider the resulting play and determine if you have increased the complexity of the call unnecessarily. As noted in figure #6, this is an example of a very complex play due to the changes in the primary play action.

As you will see, an abundance of play-call combinations can really confound a defense, but they are not complicated for a youth offense to learn. The base plays and "Air Raid" alone, out of multiple formations, create powerful attacks. When "Auburn," "Oregon," "Jet," and "Jet Dive" are added, you have a nearly complete offense that is fun to execute.

The next section gives some more pieces of the puzzle for the offense by adding new passing possibilities.

A More Complex Passing Package

While passing isn't frequent in this offense, with older youth around 12+ in age, it is possible to increase the frequency of passing to a larger degree. If younger teams pass about 20% of the time, older teams can handle, with the right QB, as much as 30%. Therefore, the opportunity to give a different look to confound a defense cannot be ignored.

When considering a more advanced passing attack for a youth team, think about *ease* of the following:

- o   The team's executing the play.
- o   The team's remembering the play and pass routes.
- o   The QB's selecting the receiver. We would like to take away the need for the QB to make progressive reads and not need to worry about defensive alignment and coverages.

22 Formation and Play Action

The "22" formation gives a four (4) receiver look and provides less protection for the QB, hence its inclusion merits as the primary formation for a more complex passing package. While the plays are not significantly more complex in execution than other plays of the offense, you will need to have a solid offensive line that can hold their blocks well.

Almost all of the plays in our offensive system are play-action in nature, and when considering an advanced passing game, there is not a significant change from that philosophy. Play action can be used in every formation and "22 Arkansas Black Air Raid" is a good example as seen in the figure #1.

Execution of this play involves a change in action between the QB and FB which must be coached. If the FB is realigned, then there is no fake handoff to execute; consequently, I do not recommend FB realignment in any passing plays out of the "22" formation. In addition, even if you don't include the play action, you will want the FB in the backfield for pass protection, so realignment doesn't make sense for this reason either. If the FB is used for the fake handoff, he will also need to learn to alter his route as outlined above.

22 Arkansas Black Air Raid

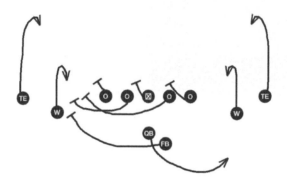

Figure #1

This play really pushes the limits of a youth team given the pass protection that is required. Introduce the "22" formation with play action later in the season. The QB and FB will need to learn a new play action and the QB, Wings, and TE's will need to remember the pass routes that are called.

To properly call a play out of the "22" formation with play action, you have two considerations:

1) Combine a play with "Air Raid." This will give the FB his alignment, identify if there is any play action, let the QB know which side of the field he will waggle, and signal which TE will be the primary receiver or,

2) Signal the FB's alignment (as discussed in an earlier chapter) as if he is to block. However, out of the "22" formation, the FB should not be re-aligned behind the Tackle, but he must remain in his original placement if you wish to use play action. The FB's alignment will also let the QB know which side of the field he is to waggle and who the primary receiver is (i.e., the QB waggles to the same side of the field that the FB is placed in the formation).

In either case, you will need to decide when using the "22" formation with "Air Raid" if you want or don't want play action. You can use "Sponge Bob" to signal "play action"/ "no play action"; the choice of the use of a special signal is entirely up to you and your team's ability to comprehend and execute.

When using the "21" or "12" formations, "Air Raid" must be combined with another play if you wish the QB to waggle to the 2-receiver side (e.g., "12 LSU Red Air Raid"). Otherwise, "Air Raid" will always have the QB waggling to the single receiver side of the formation (e.g., the side of the field with the "1" receiver).

Mirroring Routes

22 Mirror Example #1

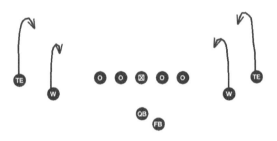

Figure #2

An aspect of a more advanced passing game is the concept of "mirroring" the TE and Wing's routes. "Mirroring" simply means that any routes run on one side of the field (e.g., "Black") are also run on the other (e.g., "Red"). Not having multiple routes means less complexity in the scheme and allows swapping the TE and Wings on one side of the formation for another. Figures #2 and #3 provide examples of a mirrored-route concept.

22 Mirror Example #2

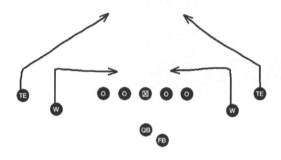

Figure #3

21 Air Raid Mirror Routes

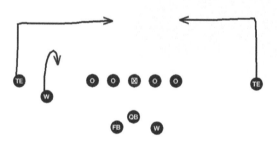

Figure #4

While we have been discussing the "22" formation, "mirroring" can also happen out of the "21" or "12" formations but only for the TE's. As an example, "21 Air Raid" has mirrored TE routes in figure #4.

Properly designed, mirrored routes may be changed in-game, but should still stay the same for each side of the field. Whatever route you call for the "Black" TE and Wing is the exact same for the "Red" TE and Wing. Those routes are pre-determined prior to game time, but they can be changed either with a time out, quarter end, or substituting a player.

Max Protect Passing

The last element that can be part of a more advanced passing game involves the use of a "max protection" pass play. The "11" formation is excellent in that it still gives the defense a three (3) receiver look but also provides three (3) additional blockers for the QB.

11 Air Raid Bob FB Red

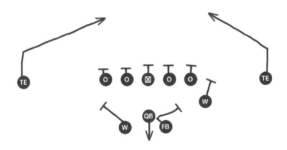

Figure #5

Figure #5 outlines "11 Georgia Red Air Raid Bob." Execution of the play does not have much play action as the QB and FB interaction is very brief. You can change that element as reflected in the play diagram if the TE's don't have enough time to get 10 yards down the field.

In this play, the QB will take a true three (3) step drop after quickly faking a handoff to the FB. This is the only play with a three-step drop, but this is necessary to give both TE's the time they need to achieve their complete 10-yard route since there is no play action involved.

Because this is a play that is a variant of "Air Raid," the signal is called using "Sponge Bob" (or whatever the signal your system uses when the play is a variant). Calling the play without using a special signal is possible but requires calling a time out, running in the play with a substitute player, or executing it when a new quarter begins.

Careful consideration should be made in selecting this play. Use it at unexpected times (e.g., first down) so the defense doesn't always assume it's a pass play in a long-yardage situation. To aid its effectiveness, run "Georgia" or "Jet Dive" out of the "11" formation a couple of times first before calling "11 Georgia Red Air Raid Bob." You **must** call either "Georgia Red" or "Georgia Black" to have the proper Wing, Strong-Side Wing, and FB alignment. The mirroring of the TE's routes is strongly suggested to aid the young QB in his passing decision.

Effective pass protection requires completion of assignments:

1. The Wing and FB should protect the QB by looking for defensive penetration in towards the offensive center on their side of the field, then work their way out towards the tackles.
2. The Strong-Side Wing should protect the C gap on his side of the field first, and then if there is no penetration, progressively back up to provide further protection for the QB.

Choosing Pass Routes

Nearly all youth defenses are not complex and don't switch between zone and man coverages. Even teams with the older players (e.g., 14+ years), don't implement much complexity with their defensive schemes. Defensive coaches often simply assign four players as CB's and Safeties (with no difference between FS and SS) and coach them to cover potential receivers. You shouldn't expect to need to change your pass routes and the overall passing scheme much if at all in-game.

The goals for the passing elements of the overall offensive scheme are twofold:

- To surprise the defense with impact plays (e.g., plays over 10 yards).

- To keep the defense honest (e.g., respecting the pass and the run alike) so the running game continues to be effective.

If you believe the defense isn't being honest, use the three guides to determine possible pass routes for the Wings and TE to create impact plays.

1) If the LB's aren't keying on the run action, are sitting 4-yards or fewer back from the Line of Scrimmage (LOS), not following the WB's or FB's, and the Safeties are staying back (8-10 yards), consider the following:
   a. Using 5-yard Curl-in routes by the Wings will be *ineffective* as the route carries the Wings into the LB's position.
   b. Having 5-yard "Out" routes for both Wings will *effectively* pull the LB's away from the middle of the field. The goal of the Wings (and their routes) is to confuse the LB's and Safeties and allow the TE's to be open as they are the primary receivers in the offense.
   c. Using 5-yard "Post" and 10-yard "Out" routes for the TE's should be *effective* as the shallow middle third or the deep outside thirds of the field should now be open.

2) If the Safeties start playing shallow (within 5-6 yards of the LOS) then consider the following:
   a. Using 10-yard Curl-in routes by the TE's *will not be effective.*
   b. Having both Wings run a "Wheel" route will *effectively* draw the Safeties to either side of the field, far away from the middle 1/3.
   c. Using 10-yard "In" or 10-yard "Post" routes should be *effective* for the TE's. This will allow them to get behind the LB's into the middle 1/3 of the field.

3) If both Safeties start playing very shallow and the LB's are not keying off the run action but staying 3-4 yards off the LOS, consider these points:
   a. To have shallow routes over the middle is desired but they will *not* be open.

     b. To counter have the Wings run 10-yard "In" routes to pull the defensive backs and LBs' into the middle third of the field.

     c. To complete the play have both TE's run 10-yard "Curl" routes, curling to the outside not inside. The outside thirds should be open.

    Note - **Scenarios 1, 2, and 3 assume using either the "21 / 12" or "22" formation and "mirroring" pass route adjustments.**

    A final note on choosing pass routes. When the TE runs a 5-yard route, consider a passing package that doesn't require play action or for the QB to waggle. The play action and having the QB waggle take time and a 5-yard route doesn't give that time to the TE. Therefore, plays such as "11 Max Protect" ("11 GA Red Air Raid Bob") or "22 Max Protect" ("22 GA Red Air Raid Bob") without play action are more appropriate for short TE routes.

Offensive Blocking

While it isn't practical to detail every aspect of offensive line and other player blocking, there are some basic principles which will make execution of the offense more effective. I could write several chapters on blocking schemes for the offensive line alone, and that's not practical for a youth offense (that doesn't practice every day). Therefore, we won't detail how to block for every defensive front, nor will we discuss every type of offensive blocking technique. However, a brief discussion for each position of some basic concepts is important. We will also discuss one popular defensive alignment, the "5-2," so the volunteer coach can have success with this offense against that alignment.

Offensive Linemen and Shoulder Blocking

In a Wing-T offense, the shoulder block is the only blocking technique that is always out of the 3-point stance for linemen. We use the shoulder block for two reasons:

- o It gives the offensive lineman more surface to strike a blow against the defender.
- o It is easier for the young lineman to hold his block longer.

When developing your practice plans, you will want to place a great deal of emphasis on offensive linemen blocking drills. You should consider some specific details:

- o Using the shoulder block and its effective technique.
- o Using the proper pulling technique and lead blocking (e.g., "gut" blocks) for the Guards.
- o Getting the offensive line not to stand up as their first motion at the snap. This is the single biggest challenge to coaching a successful young team (e.g., under 10 years old) Therefore, additional drills should be added to stop this bad habit before it begins.
- o Employing the proper technique of "down" blocking.

The Tight End, Wings, and FB

The TE's, when not split out as a receivers, should be in the 3-point stance as they are also offensive linemen. If at all possible, they should have their hand down relative to the side of the line they are aligned (e.g., if on the left side, left hand down) as well as have the same back foot slightly behind the other, shoulder length apart. This can be tough for youth players, so be patient. If they can't learn to put the correct hand down, don't push the technique. The foot placement is important so that the TE can fire off the line quickly and run out as a receiver.

When developing your practice plans, you will want to place a great deal of emphasis on TE blocking drills as follows:
o   Effective shoulder blocking.
o   Understanding and mastering "crack" blocks on defensive backs.
o   Understanding that if "Arkansas," "Oregon," "Auburn," or "LSU" is the called play to a player's side of the field, his job is to run the route as outlined by the play, blocking his man into the sideline (if a man is present) or into the middle (if no man is present). He should learn not to block into the QB or Wing's running lane (i.e., hash, numbers, and sideline).

Wing Backs will always be in the 2-point stance. They can be called to block; therefore, coaches should give special attention to effective blocking as well. He, too, uses the shoulder block as well as understands and executes two more blocks:
o   Stalk blocks
o   Crack blocks

In addition to the FB, depending on the play called, he too will shoulder block and need to master additional blocks:
o   Stalk blocks
o   Crack blocks
o   Lead blocking for the primary ball carrier.

The FB has a special role in the offense and blocking through the assigned gap will be incorporated with the section on offensive linemen and defensive fronts.

Blocking Concepts against a 5-2 Defense

Most youth teams utilize either three (3) down defensive linemen with two (2) LB's always up on the line (they may call them defensive ends or DE's), or five (5) true down defensive linemen. In both cases, they typically also have other positions:

- o Two line backers (LB's)
- o Four (4) defensive backs:
  - Two (2) corner backs (CB)
  - Two (2) safeties – a free safety (FS) and strong safety (SS). Almost all youth teams treat the roles of FS and SS as the same.

This defense is commonly called the "5-2" or some variant. Because of its popularity with youth teams, I will detail some blocking concepts to counter it.

I will focus first on the "10" formation and blocking against the 5-2. The same blocking concepts apply to its mirror, the "1" formation.

Looking at figure #1, we see the play "10 Georgia Red C":

10 Georgia Red vs. 5-2

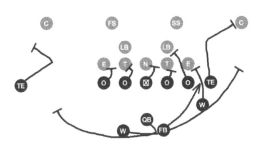

Figure #1

The important aspect to notice is the action of the Right Tackle (RT) and the Strong-Side Wing (SSW). To gain a better blocking angle, the RT ignores the DE and blocks down on the RLB. The SSW then blocks the DE, creating an inside wall. All other offensive linemen shoulder block with the head to the right if the play is going right (or left as appropriate) of the defensive linemen's head. The Strong-Side Tight End (SSTE), kicks out the corner back who would likely be covering him.

In figure #2, we see "10 Arkansas Red FB A":

10 Formation vs. 5-2

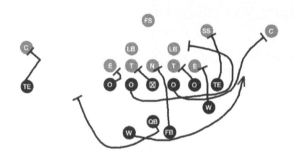

Figure #2

We have discussed the use of the pulling Guards when we detailed "Arkansas" in a previous chapter, but not their blocking assignments. When executing "Arkansas Red," players will execute the following:

1) The RG will "kick out" the Defensive Back (DB), closest to the right side line if he is present.
2) The LG will block the first LB to his inside left shoulder once he comes around the end of the line of scrimmage.
3) The RTE will block the first DB he encounters.
4) The RT (as with figure #1), and SSW's block the Right Defensive Tackle (RDT) and RDE.

Note: When executing "Arkansas Black," the blocking assignments will be the same, just on the opposite side of the field.

When the "21" or "12" formations are utilized against a 5-lineman front, a new challenge is encountered in an unblocked DE to either receiver side of the formation ("2" or "1"). Fortunately, the offense has some excellent ways to overcome this challenge by taking advantage of better angles of attack by:

- o Realigning the FB (either with or without motion) and using him to block.
- o Utilizing the SSW as a blocker without Jet Motion.
- o Using the SSW as a blocker using Jet Motion.

Figure #3 diagrams the simple means to use the DE's aggression as an advantage. In this figure the FB is realigned to the "1" receiver side of the formation, which is the direction of the primary play action for "LSU" or "Jet Black":

FB vs. DE

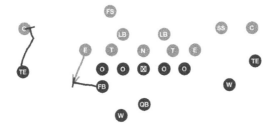

Figure #3

In figure #3 and #4 the FB allows the DE to fire up field before engaging him, creating a running lane between the FB and DE intersection just outside the LT. The FB has to simply hold the DE up so that the ball carrier can slip through the hole which is created.

If Jet Motion is used and the SSW is coming across the formation and is not the primary ball carrier, then the FB could become another lead blocker for the primary ball carrier. In this case, the SSW becomes a blocker against the DE. This scenario will be discussed later.

The Complete Offensive System for Youth Football

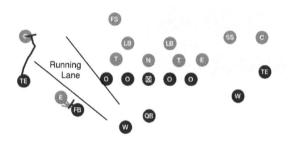

Figure #4

21 Formation vs. 5-2

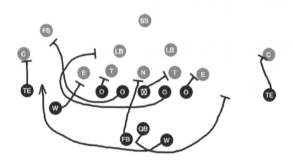

Figure #5

In figure #5 we see "21 Arkansas Black" diagrammed. The SSW, on the "2" receiver side of the formation, blocks for the Wing

102

(W), who is the primary ball carrier. The SSW will need to crack block the DE or push him away from the outside running lane.

21 Jet Red vs. DE

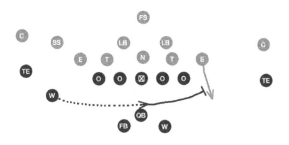

Figure #6

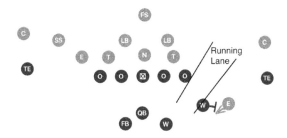

Figure #7

In figure #6 and #7 we see the SSW in Jet Motion being utilized as a blocker against the right DE. He should allow the DE to penetrate and fire up field before engaging. This will open up a hole for the primary ball carrier, typically the QB when executing "LSU Red," to that side in the same location as we saw illustrated figures #3 and #4 (when the FB was realigned and utilized as a blocker).

Use of the RG, who is pulling when executing "21 Jet Red," is also a possibility against an unblocked DE. The RG will simply let the DE penetrate, engage behind the line of scrimmage, creating a running lane similar to figure #7.

Blocking Principle of the Wing-T

Until this point in the chapter we have diagrammed ways to attack a 5-2 defense, particularly the DE's, but I didn't explain why we attacked the way we did. In figures #1 through #5 a primary principle of the Wing-T is illustrated: the use of angles to gain blocking advantages over the defense. Let's review two examples that help illustrate the principle of using angles to gain advantages.

The first example is a simple blocking scheme that is used by most youth offenses, regardless the scheme. In figure #8 we see diagrammed "10 Georgia Red C" using "simple" blocking (not our blocking scheme).

You will notice, in particular, the action of the RT and SSW is essentially, blocking the man in front of them. The SSW is not covered, so his job is to attack the LB through his gap. However, all players are essentially blocking the man that is directly across from them.

In figure #9 we see "10 Georgia Red C" using a more complicated but much more effective blocking scheme, using better attack angles. While overall most of the offensive line is making the same blocks, you will notice that the SSW and RT aren't blocking as you would typically see in a youth offense. The SSW actually has a better attack angle on the DE and can better push him away from the FB's running lane. The RT also has a better blocking angle on the outside linebacker (OLB). Not only will the RT engage the OLB faster than the Wing, his attack angle is more natural. He will be pushing back his man from an angle, rather than directly in front.

10 Georgia Red vs. 5-2 Simple

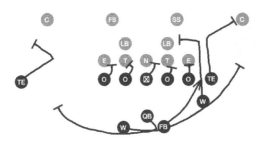

Figure #8

10 Georgia Red vs. 5-2

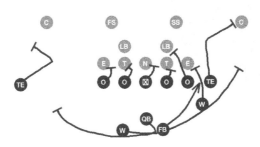

Figure #9

For another example of using angles to improve the attack, we'll diagram "1 LSU Red FB Red B." The first form of this play will be diagrammed with the more "simple" blocking technique of youth teams as seen in figure #10.

The FB will be utilized as a blocker by sending him through the "B" gap to attack the OLB. All other linemen will block the man directly in front of them.

1 LSU Red FB Red B Simple

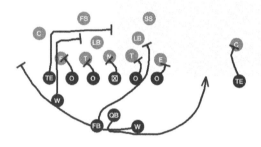

Figure #10

In figure #11, we will see an attack using improved angles. The FB is realigned and now attacks the "C" gap or the right DE. The FB will be realigned and allow the DE to penetrate somewhat into the backfield. He will then engage the DE, opening a hole between the point of attack and the RT's position. He does this by pushing the DE towards the sideline. The RT also releases and blocks the OLB at a better angle.

In both figures #10 and #11 the left TE and SSW will release into the defensive backfield to block the OLB and FS. Their angles of attack are never advantaged, but that's not important because the primary play action is far away from their position. It is possible to have the LT release and block the middle linebacker, but this would require the Wing's receiving the fake handoff to penetrate that gap as a blocker for the defensive tackle (DT). That action isn't part of the play calling scheme, but it could be introduced as a "Bob" play or a variant of "LSU."

1 LSU Red FB Red

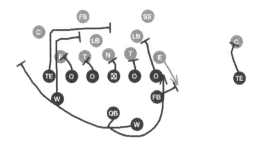

Figure #11

We have discussed a few concepts to block against the 5-2 defense as part of the standard offensive scheme. These concepts will likely be very different from any others that your league is using, so if you have returning players that didn't play in the scheme, you'll want to spend extra time "re-training" them. While time is valuable, the effort will reward itself.

Goal Line and Critical Situation Plays

The offense is designed to work well regardless of field position. However, there are situations when a completely different look, especially late in the season, can gain a tactical advantage for your team. This chapter will focus on plays that work well in goal line, short yardage, and critical situations.

Goal Line and Short Yardage

If you are within 5 yards of the goal line or 2-3 yards of a first down, these next series of plays can be very effective when employed on occasion. They are called "Power I, II and III" and are pass-oriented.

They are signaled differently than the other plays in that the play call card isn't utilized. Rather, the coach who has the primary play call board, will put the board down and make a signal: his right arm straight up for "1," both arms up (think the signal for touchdown) for "2," or both arms out like an airplane for "3." Feel free to develop your own signals.

The plays are designed to always go to the same side of the field ahead of time; that is your choice and can be changed in-game or pre-game, but the play isn't signaled each time it is called. Therefore, no play direction color is required. In addition, the formation is always the same, so no signal is needed for that either. However, a formation card can be used to signal the snap count. Other plays can be called by another coach (who is not the designated play caller) and gaps cards held up as well to create deception.

Figure #1 diagrams "Power I Black." This is a highly effective play and something similar is commonly seen with most football schemes. It is executed as follows:

1) The Black TE blocks for 1 to 2 seconds, acting as if he's being used as just an offensive lineman.
2) The Black TE then releases his block and becomes a receiver, running a 5-yard "out" route or 5-yard curl, curling out, not in.

3) The QB pivots 180 degrees and fakes a handoff to the WB, who dives through the Red A gap.
4) The QB then waggles to the Black side of the field.
5) The FB and Strong-Side Wing act as if they are blocking the Red A and B gaps respectively for the Wing.
6) The QB executes a pass to the Black TE.

Power I

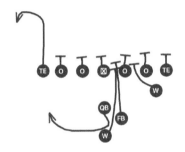

Figure #1

In the formation shown in figure #1, both TE's are on the line of scrimmage and not split out as receivers. The FB is one yard over and one yard back of the QB. The Wing is one (1) yard directly behind the QB. This is called formation "0"; there are no split wide receivers. The strong-side Wing and FB as aligned as in the "10" formation, but the Wing is aligned one (1) yards directly behind the QB.

The next play, "Power II," looks somewhat similar to "Power I" as seen in figure #2:
1) The play action is nearly identical to "Power I".
2) The QB fakes a handoff to the Wing who dives through the Red A-gap.
3) The Black TE's runs an "Out" route; the Red TE runs an "In" route. There are no delays by them blocking their man.

4) The FB will block the "C" gap, where the right TE had been.

5) The strong-side Wing goes out into the right flat as the primary receiver. That is, he runs up to the line of scrimmage and start running towards the sideline with his head and shoulders turned to his right, back towards the QB.

6) The QB "Waggles" to the Red (as diagrammed) side of the field and completes a pass to the strong-side Wing.

Note - The QB should be prepared to have a DE coming up field towards him as the TE on the Red side isn't blocking him. The FB will be making the block, but will also encounter either a LB or Safety; consequently, the QB should practice releasing his pass very quickly to the strong-side Wing.

Power II

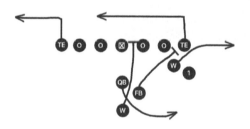

Figure #2

In "Power III" the play action is nearly identical to "Power I." Figure #3 diagrams the play. The differences between Power I and III are outlined below:

1) The QB runs a "naked boot" to the weak side (as diagrammed in figure #3, "Black" side of the field)

2) The TE's run "In" and "Out" routes respectively. That is, the left TE runs a 5-yard "in" and the right TE runs a 5-yard

"out." These routes are critical as they pull the backfield away from the QB's running lane.

Power III

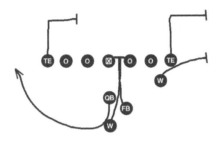

Figure #3

"Power III" or Power "I" are complimentary plays because the QB's action is the same. Execution of one play during the game can set up the other for success. run Power I a couple of times before executing Power III (or vice versa).

Ideally the "Power" series of plays should be used sparingly. However, if the defense has loaded up the LOS and you believe gaining a few yards will be exceedingly difficult, any three of the "Power" series can be successful at any time.

A Critical Situation Play

Be ready if a time in the season comes when the team encounters a critical situation: one in which winning the game is necessary for the overall success of the season. The scenario might be one of special significance: if you lose, your team doesn't make the playoffs, or won't advance in the playoffs, or is at-risk of losing the championship. "Overall success" could also be a situation that defines a losing season versus a winning season.

You'll only get one chance to execute the play because once its revealed, every team you face afterward will be looking for it. Granted, it is possible to have more trick plays. Generally, I'm not a fan of having a playbook that is trick-play heavy. I believe regular execution of gimmick plays simply makes your offense recognizable as one that regularly uses trick plays and they lose their advantage.

The next two plays are really the same play; the first play is used to set up the second play. Near the end of the season, possibly two to three games left, introduce the first play as part of your regular play-calling scheme:

- o It should be introduced and used once and no more than twice per game.
- o It should be executed early in the game, either the 1st or early 3rd quarter. This sets it up for use in the 4th quarter, when the situation is usually critical.

The first play is called "Statue I" and figure #4 diagrams it:

Statue I

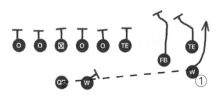

Figure #4

"Statue I" is simply a screen pass to the Wing:

1) The QB will receive the snap, turn 90 degrees to his right (or left, however you have it designated), and throw a quick pass to the Strong-Side Wing.

2) The Strong-Side Wing, once he catches the ball, yells "Go!"
3) The TE's and FB will then block for the Wing back.

The players are aligned as follows:
1) The left TE will move to the right side of the line next to the right Tackle.
2) The right TE will be on the LOS split out 8 yards from the end of the line.
3) The FB will be one yard off the LOS and two (2) yards over from the right TE, aligned as shown in figure #4
4) The strong-side Wing will be two (2) yards behind the right TE, aligned as shown in figure #4
4) The Wing will remain at the QB's right, one yard over but no yards back, to block.

"Statue I" sets up the defense by getting them accustomed to seeing this particular formation and play action. The play in and of itself is different from other plays in the offense and can be quite successful in its own right. It is, however, used only to set up the next play, "Statue II."

Statue II

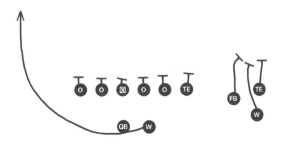

Figure #5

The Complete Offensive System for Youth Football

"Statue II," as shown in figure #5, is the actual "trick" play. If properly set up and executed, will result in a big gain and ideally a touchdown. The team should practice this play early in the season and prefect its execution. The action between the QB and Wing is special and requires deception from every player on the team. Everyone must "sell" that the strong-side Wing, acting as a receiver, has the ball. Figure #5 diagrams the play:

The play action is as follows:

1) The alignment of the TE's, FB, Wing, and strong-side Wing are identical to "Statue I".
2) The QB will receive the snap, turn 90 degrees to his right, and fake a pass to the strong-side Wing. He will make the complete passing motion, with the ball in his hand, towards the strong-side Wing.
3) The strong-side Wing, jumps up like the pass was a little high (this helps sell the fake) and yells "Go!"
4) The TE and FB will then block for the strong-side Wing back as he advances as if he as the ball.
5) Once the QB fakes the throw, he brings his right arm down by his side. He should still be facing the side-line.
6) The Wing will then walk behind the QB (who is facing the sideline), by his right hand, take the ball out of his hand, and proceed on his route as diagrammed.

Every player must act as if a screen pass was executed. No player should look back to the QB or Wing to watch the execution. Everyone should be facing forward as if the Strong-Side Wing has received a pass and proceed to block accordingly. The only player not looking at the String-Side Wing is the Wing who is walking behind the QB. Lastly, the Wing must act very calmly about the play. He must act "carefree," as if he has no concerns with what's happening with the play. Even the coaches should be looking at the Strong-Side Wing as if he caught the football. It's a total team effort to make Statue II work.

Both Statue I and Statue II are called after a timeout, a change of possession, spiking the football, and etc. This play is not called from the play call card or signaled, although they could be using only

114

"Sponge Bob" with no other play for Statue I and 'Sponge Bob Sponge Bob" for Statue II. We started the first quarter with Statue I, so no signal was needed.

You have everything you need for success: the base, expanded, variants, combined, increased passing complexity, goal line and special situation plays – a complete offensive system. You have some blocking concepts that will be effective against the 5-2, a popular youth defense. In the next chapter we will put everything together to help have success once the season begins.

Putting it All Together

You don't need to spend an inordinate amount of time (e.g., several hours) preparing for each game. If you practice well and perfect the action between the QB, FB, and Wings, as well as blocking schemes for your offensive line, then you have prepared the team offensively. However, your play-calling is really helped by having a game plan prepared ahead of time. A game plan also helps other coaches call plays if you aren't available.

Game Plan

Because a good coach shares his game plan, the complexity of it should be appropriate for the age of players you are coaching. Figure #1 illustrates a portion of a basic plan that might be used a couple of games into the season:

#	Dn	Dist	Formation	Play	Dir	Gap	FB Lead Block	Motion	Re-Align FB
1	1	10	10	GA	R	A	N		
2	2	8	1	AR	B	A	N		
3	3	3	11	GA Bob	R	C	Y		
4	4	1	1	LSU	R	A	N		
5	1	10	12	AR	R		Y	FB Black to Red	Black
6	2	8	21	Jet	R	A	N	Jet Red	
7	3	2	11	LSU	B	A	N		
8	4	1	21	GA	B	C	N		
9	1	10	22	Jet Dive	B	A	N	Jet Black	
10	2	10	11	Arkansas – Air Raid	R		Y		Black
11	3	3	1	GA Bob	B	C	Y		
12	4	1	12	Jet Black – LSU Red	R	A	N	Jet Black	
13	1	10	12	Auburn	R			FB Auburn	
14	2	10	21	Auburn – Air Raid	B			FB Auburn	
15	3	2	1	Arkansas Black	B		Y	FB Red to Black	Red
16	4	1	22	GA	R	C	N		

Figure #1

The plan can be made using any number of spreadsheet applications or even drawn by hand. When creating your plan, you will want to make it so that calling plays from it are easy and fast. Once printed, you'll want to laminate both sides in case of inclement weather.

Referring back to figure #1:

o The first column is the "Play #." You can call plays based on this sequence, or ignore it all together. For example, your first play is #1, your second play is #2, and etc.

o The second column is the "Down." Again, you can call in sequence or use this column to help you determine when to call a particular play. For example, 1st down plays are called on 1st down only, 2nd down plays are called on 2nd down only, and etc. Again, it's up to you.

o The third column in the "Distance" in yards the offense needs to gain for a first down. You can call a play based on need. For example, if the distance is short (<3 yards) and the down is 4th, then you might run "Georgia." If the distance is long (10+) and the down is 2nd, you might call "21 Auburn Air Raid."

o The fourth column is the "Direction" of the primary action – Left/Right or "Black/Red." On this particular game plan sheet, where the play is "combined," the color will always be the first play, not the second. You can modify it for your game plan and make the color the second play if needed, but it helps us to recognize when FB motion takes place.

o The fifth column is the dive or blocking "Gap" for the FB or primary ball carrier (as appropriate). More often than not we default to "A." The actual gap can be changed in game based on how the offensive line is blocking, defensive alignment, and other factors.

o The sixth column identifies if the FB should be signaled to block. A "Y" indicates he is signaled to block.

o The seventh column is the type of motion on the play, either the FB or Jet. Remember, if you don't re-align your FB to block opposite the primary ball carriers route, then there should be no FB motion identified.

- o The eighth column identifies where to locate the FB if he is realigned to block. Note - There should be no motion if the FB is aligned to the same side as the primary ball carrier's route or if the play is "Auburn," "Oregon," or "Jet."

If your game plan allows you to understand the play call and action with that level of detail quickly, then it should be sufficient for your team. If calling the plays requires a great deal of thinking or hesitation, then you will need to simplify whatever detail you have developed. The game plan should be changed as you learn more about how your team, as well as your competition, executes.

Play Call Sheet

Even having a game plan developed is often not enough should you need to deviate in the game or if another coach is calling the plays. I suggest having a play-call sheet handy. This is a sheet that diagrams the plays in base form only, along with suitable formations for each play, but it does not include combined plays. Figure #2 details an old play call sheet we used (not current).

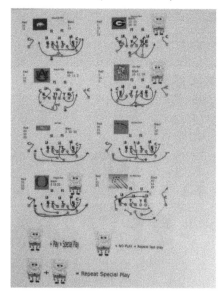

Figure #2

The call sheet in Figure #2 shows only the "Red" version of each play out of the base formations (either "10" or "1"), so the plays can fit on one page. However, you could create one that has the "Black" plays on the backside, variants, or even combined plays if needed. I decided I didn't need that complexity.

Your play-call sheet can be created with any number of free drawing programs or simply drawn by hand. Once it is made, you will want to also laminate it on both sides.

Chalkboard Sheet

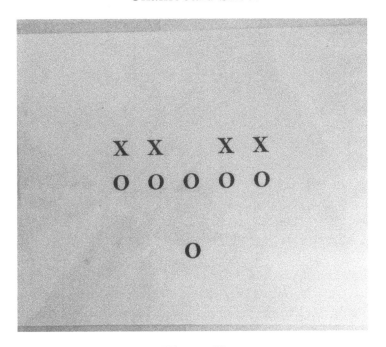

Figure #3

Once you have a game plan and play call sheet, you'll want to be able to make adjustments during the game, and then communicate those to the team. Figure #3 shows a blank laminated "chalkboard" sheet. This sheet shows the placement of the offensive line and QB minus the Wings and TE's; it can be on the back of the Play Call Sheet. It's laminated so you can use a dry erase marker to quickly write on it and erase as needed. Since the offensive line and QB positions never change, regardless of formation, they are preprinted on the sheet. The other positions are written in as needed. Figure #4 shows how a sheet might look with adjustments hastily written during a game.

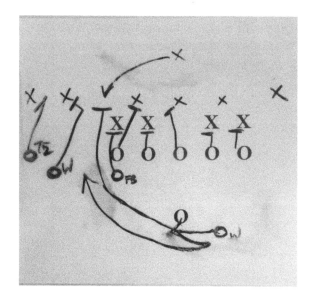

Figure #4

Adjustments and Setting Expectations

As a coach you make adjustments on several elements: overall offensive production, a specific play, or even a series of plays. Before each game, jot them down on the game plan. Because the players need to clearly understand, you should also communicate your expectations to the team and get their "buy in."

When to adjust a play or even the entire offensive scheme is the tricky part of coaching and is what separates the good from the great. You don't want to overreact and make adjustments too fast. Conversely, waiting too long is a problem as well; be patient and prudent. Wait until you've run the same play at least three times before deciding that it is not "working."

Knowing "when" is only part of what makes the decision tricky; you must also know "why" and "what." That is, when expectations aren't being met, you need to have a firm reasoning: "why" they aren't being met and then know "what" you are going to do to fix it.

When a play, or the offense in general, isn't meeting expectations, key places to examine before deciding what to do:

- o Pay special attention to the blocking assignments and the offensive line in particular. Often when a play continues to break down, there is a misunderstanding regarding a blocking assignment.
- o Focus on Wings and TE's blocking. These are often an area for improvement. Those two positions can get sloppy as they don't block on every play.
- o Look for excellent execution among the QB, FB, and Wings, that is, the primary play action sequence. If the timing of the action between the QB, FB, and Wings is sloppy, if fakes aren't crisp and believable, the entire offense will suffer.
- o Gage the timing of the handoff and fake handoff with the Jet Sweep and Jet Dive plays. This is critical. If the Wing in motion is just a little late or a little early, the sequence of handoffs or fakes won't work and will create problems. Focus on this action closely for poor execution.
- o Watch the timing and execution of the pitching action from QB to Wing when running "Auburn." This, too, is vital to success. You will want to practice pitches going to the left and right with both Wings.
- o Keep a close eye on the action between the Strong-Side-Wing and QB when running "Oregon," which requires a very good fake at full speed to make it a successful play and look for failures.
- o Watch for the Wing or FB to pause or even make a slight "jump" when receiving the handoff in the primary play sequence. This is a big no-no as it creates timing problems and is a key for the defense that the handoff is real.

Sometimes, despite patiently watching the offense, you realize that you are out-manned. That is, your players simply can't block their assignments, catch their passes, or outrun the defense because the other team is more athletic on that day for whatever reason. In

The Complete Offensive System for Youth Football

those cases, do the best you can and then regroup. It happens. Whatever you do, don't get angry with the kids; they still want to have fun.

Setting up the Defense

The overall system and all plays in it are designed to attack the gut, off-tackle and the flanks, primarily by using the running game:

- o "Georgia," "Jet Dive," and "Georgia Bob" attack the gut and off-tackle.

- o "Arkansas," "Auburn," "Oregon,", "LSU", and "Jet" attack the flanks.

- o "Air Raid" is added to keep the defense guessing and honest, so that the overall running game remains effective.

Each series of plays is created to complement each other. When calling your plays, you will use them to set up the defense. You are trying to make them position and react in a way that will cause them to be counter-productive. Look at a few ways to setup the defense and make the game more complicated for them:
1) The first way you do this is to change up your formations after a series:
   - o Start with "1," "10," and "11"
   - o Then add in "12" and "21." You have gotten more complex simply with formation changes.
   - o While we haven't discussed "20" or "2," these are two excellent formations that can be used late in the season to provide a very different look.
2) "Air Raid" to the 2-receiver side of the "21" or "12" formation can be very effective since most of the season teams haven't seen it used in this way (remember, we typically send the QB to the weak side or "1" receiver side of the field). Therefore, call some plays that go back to this side of the formation (e.g., if using a "21" formation call "21 LSU Black Air Raid").

3) Repeated attacks to one area, on both sides of the field, will set up the defense for another attack it's not ready to counter:
   o Run "Arkansas," "LSU," and "Jet Sweep" a few times to attack the flanks.
   o When you see the defense starting to cheat their safeties or LB's to the outside, run "Georgia," "Georgia Bob," or "Jet Dive." Just as the defense settles in and defends the flanks, the middle opens up and the FB or the Wing (with the FB lead blocking) will have a nice gain. Then, reverse your attack.
   o Run "Georgia," "Jet Dive," and "Georgia Bob" several times. As the middle becomes congested, execute "LSU," "Oregon," or "Auburn" and hit the flanks with a whole new look.
   o Once you have them focused on the run, call Air Raid to loosen them back up.
   o After you have them unsettled, they will start "keying" on each play's action and will start getting smarter with their attack. At that time, you then combine a play like "21 Auburn Air Raid" or "12 Arkansas Red LSU Black FB Black." The primary play action will result in the defense heading the wrong direction. Combined plays executed when the defense becomes comfortable are usually very effective.

Be patient and execute consistent attacks before calling a new attack. When you see the defense becoming accustomed to one particular attack, that's the time you change things up.

Conclusion

This concludes our scheme. I would encourage you in your first season to stick to everything as closely as possible as outlined in this book. Once you are comfortable with the scheme and its elements, you can start adding your own flavor. I believe if you are the only coach running this scheme that you will have the best on-field offensive success in your league – the kids are really going to have fun!

You might need to read through the material a couple of times before taking the scheme to the field. Have a number of points completely ingrained (at a minimum):

1. Know the characteristics of a good coach.
2. Be comfortable with calling plays for this hurry-up-no-huddle offense. You should know how to quickly communicate the play, formation, gaps, and FB blocking assignments.
3. Understand the scheme design and how it attacks a defense.
4. Execute the three base and first passing play with perfection.
5. Effectively use the FB to block.
6. Execute more complex plays involving the use of the option, jet motion, and the fake reverse.
7. Understand how to add variants to a few plays and communicate them to the offense on the field
8. Know how to combine plays to create a high level of offensive complexity that your youth team will have no difficulty understanding.
9. Understand how to add more passing complexity for older teams.
10. Know what to do in short yardage and critical situations when your offense stalls.
11. Plan your game in general and play calling in particular.

In closing remember most of all that you want the kids to have fun and for you to be an inspiration!

Appendix A – Additional Resources

I have no affiliation and derive no income from these resources in any way. These are simply resources I have found that have been helpful for me personally.

Websites:

www.wingt.com
(One of the best Wing-T websites. Much is free, but a subscription will get you even more).

www.Bucksweep.com
(Gives a good general overview of the Wing-T offensive system)

www.Youthfootballonline.com
(Videos, drills, playbooks, and other resources)

www.Coacheschoice.com
(Great website for nearly every book or video you could ever want about anything regarding a variety of sports – a huge assortment for football)

www.Footballxos.com

www.Coachhuey.com
(Message board for coaches at all levels)

www.Footballcoachingsites.com

Note - don't get overwhelmed or try to complicate things with your team after visiting the websites!

iPad App – "Coachme Football Edition" (used to draw and execute plays – very good)

The Complete Offensive System for Youth Football

Drills - "Racehorse Practice Drills – The Complete Wing-T Drill Book" – Dennis Creehan (this is the Bible for Wing-T football drills) This is an e-book that can be difficult to locate.

Drawing/Illustrating Programs – GIMP (for iMac) and Paint.Net (PC)

GIMP can be found at https://www.gimp.org

Paint.Net can be found at http://www.getpaint.net/index.html

These programs were used to create play-call sheets and edit pictures for play/formation cards. They are freeware, but a donation is recommended.

There are a host of free images for your play cards which can found using Google, DuckDuckGo, and other web search engines.

Appendix B – List of Possible Plays

This is not an exhaustive list of all possible plays, but it can help you prepare your game plan:

- Table #1 details only one side's formation, since each play is a mirror executed with another formation (e.g., "10" and "1").
- As best as possible, effective combined plays will be listed, although there are possible combinations that are not listed.
- The table details: the play name and direction, if motion is possible (for "Jet," "Auburn," and "Oregon" motion always exists), if the play is a standard, variant (as we have them), or a combined type, if the FB can be re-aligned, if the FB can motion, if he is to motion where to place him based on the called play, and any important notes to the play that you would need to consider for successful execution.

You will not use 85% of these plays and don't be tempted to do so either. If you took the possible number of plays and their "mirrors," there are well over 100 and that's not practical for a youth offense to memorize. Remember to practice any plays that have changes to the primary play action between the QB, FB and Wings!

Table #1

#	For-mation	Play	Potential Motion	Play Type	Can FB Re-align?	Can FB Motion?	For Motion Place FB	Important Notes
1	10	Arkansas Red	Yes	Standard	Y	Y	Black	
2	10	Georgia Red		Standard	N	N		
3	10	LSU Black	Yes	Standard	Y	Y	Red	
4	10	LSU - Bob	Yes	Variant	Y	Y	Black	QB follows Wing and FB to the Red side of the field

The Complete Offensive System for Youth Football

#	For-mation	Play	Potential Motion	Play Type	Can FB Re-align?	Can FB Motion?	For Motion Place FB	Important Notes
5	10	Arkansas Red - LSU Red	Yes	Combined	Y	Y	Black	
6	10	Arkansas Red - LSU Black	Yes	Combined	Y	Y	Red	
7	10	Arkansas Red - Air Raid	Yes	Combined	Y	Y	Red	
8	10	Air Raid	Yes	Standard	Y	Y	Red	
9	10	Georgia - Bob		Variant	N	N		Wing receives handoff and follows FB through called gap
10	11	Arkansas Red	Yes	Standard	Y	Y	Black	
11	11	Georgia Red		Standard	N	N		
12	11	LSU Black	Yes	Standard	Y	Y	Red	
13	11	LSU - Bob - FB Red		Variant	Y	N		Must call out FB position for proper formation alignment
14	11	Arkansas Red - LSU Red	Yes	Combined	Y	Y	Black	
15	11	Arkansas Red - LSU Black	Yes	Combined	Y	Y	Red	
16	11	Arkansas Red - Air Raid	Yes	Combined	Y	Y	Red	
17	11	Air Raid - FB Red		Standard	Y	N		Must call out FB blocking direction for proper formation alignment
18	11	Georgia - Bob		Variant	N	N		Wing receives handoff and follows FB through called gap
19	11	Jet Black	Yes	Standard	Y	N		SSW should know his place in formation based on call
20	11	Air Raid – Max Protect	Yes	Standard	Y	Y	Red or Black	**Can also be called as as 'Georgia Red – Air Raid Bob"** Since this isn't a combined play, FB motion will need to be a "Bob" variant. There is no way to signal FB motion.
21	21	Arkansas Black	Yes	Standard	Y	Y	Red	
22	21	Georgia Red		Standard	N	N		

128

Pat Moss

#	For-mation	Play	Potential Motion	Play Type	Can FB Re-align?	Can FB Motion?	For Motion Place FB	Important Notes
23	21	LSU Red	Yes	Standard	Y	Y	Black	
24	21	LSU - Bob	Yes	Variant	Y	Y	Red	
25	21	Oregon Black	Yes	Standard	Y	N		
26	21	Auburn Black	Yes	Standard	N	Y	FB motion Part of Play	
27	21	Auburn Black - Air Raid	Yes	Combined	N	Y	FB motion Part of Play	
28	21	Oregon Black - Air Raid	Yes	Combined	Y	N		
29	21	Arkansas Black - Air Raid	Yes	Combined	Y	Y	Black	
30	21	Arkansas Black - LSU Black	Yes	Combined	Y	Y	Red	
31	21	Jet Red	Yes	Standard	Y	N		
32	21	Jet Red Dive	Yes	Standard	N	N		
33	21	Jet Red - Arkansas Black	Yes	Combined	Y	N		
34	21	Jet Red - Arkansas Red	Yes	Combined	Y	N		
35	21	Jet Red - LSU Black	Yes	Combined	Y	N		
36	21	Jet Red - LSU Red	Yes	Combined	Y	N		
37	21	Jet Red - Air Raid	Yes	Combined	Y	N		
38	21	Georgia Red - LSU Red	Yes	Combined	Y	Y	Black	
39	21	Georgia Red - LSU Black	Yes	Combined	Y	Y	Red	
40	22	Air Raid - FB Red	No	Standard	Y	N		Must call out FB blocking direction for proper formation alignment
41	21	Oregon – Bob	Yes	Combined	N	N		**Also known as "21 Oregon – Georgia Red Bob" – A Dive play**

The Complete Offensive System for Youth Football

#	Formation	Play	Potential Motion	Play Type	Can FB Re-align?	Can FB Motion?	For Motion Place FB	Important Notes
42	21	Auburn - Bob	Yes	Combined	N	Y	Part of Play	Also known as "21 Auburn Black – GA Red Bob" – A Dive play – Wing receives handoff

Note: There is no mirror of the "22" formation. However, the plays themselves can be mirrored within the formation itself (i.e., Jet Black Dive can also be called Jet Red Dive and etc.)

#	Formation	Play	Potential Motion	Play Type	Can FB Re-align?	Can FB Motion?	For Motion Place FB	Important Notes
43	22	Jet Black	Yes	Standard	Y	N		
44	22	Jet Black Dive	Yes	Standard	N	N		
45	22	Air Raid Max Protect	No	Standard	Y	Y	Red or Black	Can also be called as as 'Georgia Red – Air Raid Bob" Since this isn't a combined play, FB motion will need to be a "Bob" variant. There is no way to signal FB motion.
46	22	Jet Black – Air Raid	Yes	Combined	Y	N		
47	22	Jet Black – LSU Black	Yes	Combined	Y	N		Not recommended to re-align the FB – FB will need to know that the QB's route is Black and be prepared to block to the Black side
48	22	Jet Black Dive – LSU Black	Yes	Combined	N	N		FB receives a fake handoff after the fake handoff to the Wing in Jet motion.
49	22	Jet Black – LSU Red	Yes	Combined	Y	N		Not recommended to re-align the FB – FB will need to know that the QB's route is Red and be prepared to block to the Red side

Note: The "20"and "2" formations weren't discussed much, but are good formations to show a different look to the defense. Nearly every play can be run with "20" or "2". The exceptions are any "Air Raid" plays with the QB Waggling to the "1" receiver side of the formation. The TE on that side of the formation isn't split out. Therefore, the 5 and 10-yard Post & In routes are not recommended for this player out of this formation. The following are a small sampling of plays out of the "20" formation.

#	Formation	Play	Potential Motion	Play Type	Can FB Re-align?	Can FB Motion?	For Motion Place FB	Important Notes
50	20	LSU Red	Yes	Standard	Y	Y	Black	
51	20	Arkansas Black – LSU Red	Yes	Combined	Y	Y	Black	
52	20	Georgia Black	No	Standard	N	N		
53	20	Air Raid	Yes	Standard	Y	Y	Black	Use either Curl (Out) our Out Routes
54	20	Jet Red	Yes	Standard	Y	N		
55	20	Jet Red Dive	Yes	Standard	N	N		

Pat Moss

#	For-mation	Play	Potential Motion	Play Type	Can FB Re-align?	Can FB Motion?	For Motion Place FB	Important Notes
56	20	Jet Red – Air Raid	Yes	Combined	Y	N		Use either Curl (Out) our Out Routes
57	0	Power I	No	Standard	Y	Y	Red	FB realignment and motion not recommended, but possible
58	0	Power II	No	Standard	Y	Y	Black	FB realignment and motion not recommended, but possible
59	0	Power III	No	Standard	Y	Y	Red	FB realignment and motion not recommended, but possible
60	3	Statue 1	No	Standard	N	N		
61	3	Statue 2	No	Standard	N	N		

Glossary

Black – the left side of the field starting at the center's left arm in this scheme.

Dive – a running play through the offensive line gaps A, B, and occasionally C in this scheme (e.g., 1, 3, and 5 or 2, 4, and 6 in the standard offensive gap numbering system). There is almost never a lead blocker in this scheme except on "variant" plays (e.g., "Georgia Bob") of this type.

Flank – the areas to the left or right sides of the offensive line on either side of the tackle or tight end (if he's not split out)

Full Back – a potential ball carrier that is one yard over and one yard back of the QB in the standard formations. He can also be aligned two yards directly behind an offensive tackle.

Gut – any interior line gaps (not outside the TE). The running gaps A, B, and occasionally C in this scheme only (e.g., 1, 3, and 5 or 2, 4, and 6 in the standard offensive gap numbering system).

Jet Motion – pre-snap motion, executed by a Strong-Side Wing or Wing back, that is very fast and across the line of scrimmage, and going either left-to-right or right-to-left. The Wing runs parallel to the line of scrimmage.

Line of Scrimmage – One of two vertical planes parallel to the goal line when the ball is to be put in play. The line of scrimmage is through the point of the ball closest to their end line.

Motion – a player moving across the field, facing the opposite sideline, before the ball is snapped, but after the QB has said, "Set."

Pulling Guard – an offensive lineman in the guard position that leaves his position and travels around the end of the offensive line as a lead blocker.

Red – the right side of the field starting at the center's right arm in this scheme.

Splits – the distance between the feet of one offensive linemen to the feet of the next offensive lineman or receiver.

Strong-Side Wing – a potential ball carrier or blocker that is one yard over and one yard back of the offensive tackle. Usually in this position the player is a blocker, but can be a receiver as well as a ball carrier.

Strong-Side Wing Back – See Strong-Side Wing

Tight End – the last offensive lineman on the left or right on the offensive line. He is always to the left or right of the offensive tackle on each side of the offensive line. He may be used as a receiver or as a blocker in this position.

Waggle – a "naked bootleg" - a running path the QB takes with no lead blocker; used in pass plays in the scheme.

Wing – a potential ball carrier or blocker that is two yards over and one yard back of the QB. A Wing may also be the placed into the slot receiver position, one yard back and six yards over off the line of scrimmage.

Wing Back – See Wing

Wide Receiver – a TE that is slid out six (6) to eight (8) yards depending on the called formation.